The Marketing Strategy Desktop Guide

Second edition

Norton Paley

THOROGOOD

Thorogood Publishing
10-12 Rivington Street
London EC2A 3DU

Telephone: 020 7749 4748
Fax: 020 7729 6110
Email: info@thorogoodpublishing.co.uk
Web: www.thorogoodpublishing.co.uk

© Norton Paley 2007

A CIP catalogue record for this book is
available from the British Library.

ISBN PB: 978-185418490-0
RB: 978-185418491-7

Printed in the UK by Ashford Colour Press.

Designed and typeset in the UK by Driftdesign.

Special discounts for bulk
quantities of Thorogood books
are available to corporations,
institutions, associations and
other organisations. For more
information contact Thorogood
by telephone on 020 7749 4748, by
fax on 020 7729 6110, or e-mail us:
info@thorogoodpublishing.co.uk

Dedication

To my family and especially to Annette – my wife, friend,
and good-natured editor.

About the author

Norton Paley has over 25 years of corporate experience in general management, marketing management and product development at McGraw-Hill Inc, John Wiley & Sons and Alexander-Norton Inc. He has authored the following books:

- The Strategic Marketing Planner
- Action Guide to Marketing Planning and Strategy
- Marketing for the Non-marketing Executive: An Integrated Management Resource Guide
- The Marketing Strategy Desktop Guide
- Pricing Strategies and Practices
- Marketing Principles and Tactics Everyone Must Know
- The Manager's Guide to Competitive Strategies, 2nd Ed.
- Successful Business Planning
- Manage to Win

In addition to advising management on competitive strategies and strategic planning, Paley also has extensive global experience lecturing to managers at such firms as American Express, Cargill (worldwide), Chevron Chemical, Babcock & Wilcox, Dow Chemical (worldwide), W.R. Grace & Co., Prentice-Hall, Ralston-Purina, Hoechst, and McDonnell-Douglas. Also, he participated in lecture tours in the Republic of China and Mexico.

His byline columns have appeared in The Management Review and Sales & Marketing Management.

Icons

Throughout the Desktop Guide series of books you will see references and symbols in the margins. These are designed for ease of use and quick reference directing you to key features of the text. The symbols used are:

 case study

 best practice

 for example

Contents

Introduction   **1**

1   **How to manage marketing in the 21st century**   **7**

Chapter objectives 8

Marketing successes 11

Marketing strategy 14

Strategy teams 19

Identifying opportunities 21

Best practices 22

2   **How to manage your marketing strategy (Part 1)**   **25**

Chapter objectives 26

Primary strategy principles 27

Strategy applications 32

A focus on marketing strategy 41

Best practices 43

3   **How to manage your marketing strategy (Part 2)**   **45**

Chapter objectives 46

Part 1 – Marketing mix 51

Part 2 – External forces 53

Best practices 61

4   **How to manage your competitor intelligence**   **63**

Chapter objectives 64

Information, intelligence and decision-making 64

Developing a competitor intelligence system..................................67

Competitor intelligence model...68

Strategy applications 70

Marketing research techniques 73

Types of data 74

Generating primary data 75

Use agents to improve competitive intelligence results 86

Best practices 89

5 How to manage your strategic marketing plans   91

Chapter objectives 92

The strategic marketing plan: a document for success 97

Marketing plan: one year 105

Best practices 108

6 How to manage your markets: The power of segmentation   109

Chapter objectives 110

Segmentation in action 110

Select a market segment 114

Eight additonal segment categories to pinpoint
markets for greater accuracy 117

Portfolio analysis 122

Strength/weakness analysis 132

Best practices 137

7 How to manage your product strategy   139

Chapter objectives 140

Product life cycle 143

Product competition 149

Product mix 150

Product design 151

New products/ services 153

Product audit 162

Best practices 167

8 | **How to manage your communications strategy** | **169**

Chapter objectives..170

Developing a successful advertising campaign 172

Determining your advertising budget..176

Guidelines for successful sales promotion 179

How to use sales promotion to stimulate sales 181

Marketing over the Internet..187

Best practices 191

9 | **How to manage your pricing strategy** | **193**

Chapter objectives..194

Sales forecasting..194

Pricing new products 201

Pricing strategies...204

Pricing established products 207

Pricing guidelines 211

Best practices 212

10 | **How to manage your distribution strategy** | **213**

Chapter objectives..214

Channel commitment..214

Channel coverage...216

Distribution and market exposure..220

Direct versus indirect distribution...222

Making the channel decision 226

Channel control 227

Selecting distributors..227

Evaluating distributors 231

Best practices 234

11

How to think like a strategist   **235**

Chapter objectives 236

Leadership and implementing strategy 237

Relationship marketing 240

Align marketing strategy with your corporate culture 241

Benchmarking for success 245

Think like a strategist 247

Best practices 249

Introduction

'If you don't have a strategy, you will be permanently reactive and part of somebody else's strategy', declared the well-known futurist, Alfred Toffler.

The statement is loaded with innuendoes of dire circumstances. It implies a reprimand for not having a strategy. Yet, it also promises great outcomes for having one.

Consider this notion of strategy in the following examples. Would you regard these business successes as reactive, or a matter of chance? Or was there an underlying strategy influencing each achievement?

- Lego plastic toy blocks were first introduced in 1949. Since then slightly more than 203 billion have been made. Invented by Ole Kirk Christiansen, a master carpenter from Denmark, there are now 2,000 different Lego elements, and Lego theme parks in Britain, Denmark, and the U.S.

- The lowly paper clip does not seem much in the world of technology. Yet, this universal desk necessity, invented by Norwegian Johan Vaaler in 1900, replaced the straight pin to secure papers. Vaaler, however, didn't realize its great potential and sold the patent to Gem Manufacturing, a British stationer, that made it a striking market success.

- The first version of the modern vacuum cleaner was invented in 1907 by James Murray Spangler. After trying unsuccessfully to market his invention, Spangler joined with William Hoover. Thus, the Hoover Company was born – and so was a marketing success, making Hoover a household word.

- The paperback book was the brainy idea of Allen Lane, managing director of the British publishing house Bodley Head. After scanning the news stand for something to read and finding only magazines and reprints of Victorian novels, Lane hit upon the idea of the portable book. The first ten paperbacks – appearing under the imprint Penguin – which were introduced in 1935, included the works of Agatha Christie and Ernest Hemingway.

- The safety razor of today had its beginning in 1895 when King Camp Gillette realized there might be a market for a razor with a disposable blade. It took him eight years to develop the blade and start production. But it was only during World War I that the product took off when Gillette supplied 3.5 million razors and 36 million blades to U.S. soldiers. In turn, that fortuitous move created a substantial base of customers who kept coming back for refills long after the Treaty of Versailles.

Were those business classics just a matter of coming up with the product idea and letting the 'world beat a path to its door'?

Or, more accurately, was there a unified effort by an individual or a company to reach a target audience with a product that solved a problem or satisfied a perceived need or want; priced so that it conveyed value for services provided; distributed in a convenient form and in a reasonable timeframe to the customer; and promoted through media that informed and educated prospects about the product?

The answer is a resounding 'yes' to indicate that marketing success doesn't just happen. A plan is needed to house the information about internal operations and competencies, strategies to reach markets and deliver products, and tactics to initiate precise actions for pricing and promotions.

The current emphasis on the Internet presents vastly different situations from what existed during the timeframes of the above case examples. For instance, managers now face an increasing number of global competitors. Internet entrepreneurs leap into so-called secure markets and whisk away once loyal customers. Mind-boggling new technology harnesses innovative products customized for customers, and new forms of communications connect sellers to waiting customers with amazing speed.

That's not all. There are also the effects of changing demographics, shifting lifestyles, fragmented cultural markets, and shortened product life cycles that add to the complexity of devising winning marketing strategies.

Thus, the central aim of this desktop guide is to arm you with the best practices from the winning companies of the past few decades and to provide pragmatic guidelines to help you develop competitive marketing strategies.

You can use this desktop guide in two ways:

1. You can read the guide cover-to-cover and acquire the basic concepts, explanations and techniques for planning and implementing competitive marketing strategies in an organized and logical flow.

2. You can jump into the guide at any chapter that interests you and receive mental nourishment and stimulation to tackle your business problems with fresh energy and new ideas. Within each chapter you will find numerous step-by-step guidelines

and actual company examples to provide practical assistance for your business. For example:

Chapter 1: identifies the driving forces that will impact competitive marketing strategies in a competitive global marketplace. You will also find a systematic approach to search for fresh market opportunities.

Chapter 2: outlines the historical roots of strategy and relates them to new business practices in a global economy. You will learn how to employ the five primary strategy principles that are inherent in most marketing actions.

Chapter 3: shows how to devise competitive strategies to outperform competitors. Further, guidelines indicate how to use the marketing mix as a resource for developing strategies and tactics.

Chapter 4: reveals how to apply competitive intelligence techniques to manage your market position. You will learn how to use the basic methods of primary data collection and how to employ agents to augment traditional intelligence approaches.

Chapter 5: presents the strategic marketing plan. You will learn planning techniques to develop a strategic direction, objectives and strategies, and a portfolio of products and markets.

Chapter 6: displays the techniques for segmenting a market. You will see how to use the major screening approaches to evaluate a market segment as well as conduct a strength/weakness analysis for your business.

Chapter 7: uses a framework of six major factors to develop product strategies. You will learn how to use product life cycle guidelines to revitalize sales and extend the sales life of your products and you can make use of a product audit to sustain product profitability.

Chapter 8: shows how to develop a successful advertising campaign, use sales promotion to stimulate sales, and identify ways to utilize the Internet.

Chapter 9: identifies the primary sales forecasting techniques used in pricing. It reveals how to apply the five pricing strategies for new products and the six pricing strategies for established products.

Chapter 10: presents the primary strategies for moving a product to its intended market. You are shown the criteria for choosing channels of distribution and techniques for evaluating supply-chain performance.

Chapter 11: defines the leadership role of the manager in the Internet age. You will see how to align marketing strategies with your corporate culture and use relationship marketing for optimum efficiency in a customer-driven marketplace. And you will learn how to install procedures to benchmark your marketing strategy and improve performance.

Finally, and most meaningful, this desktop guide promises that you will learn how to *think* and *act* like a strategist.

1

How to manage marketing
in the 21st century

Chapter objectives

Marketing successes

Marketing strategy

Strategy teams

Identifying opportunities

Best practices

Chapter objectives

After reading this chapter you should be able to:

1. **Identify the driving forces that will impact competitive marketing strategy in a competitive global marketplace.**

2. **Define the duties and responsibilities of a strategy team and use it as a support structure for your organization.**

3. **Use a systematic approach to find fresh market opportunities.**

What distinguishing features characterize the marketing function, and in particular marketing strategy, in the 21st century?

To a great measure, the answers to those formidable questions were taking shape during the last two decades of the 20th century through a continuous string of momentous events. For instance:

- Intensifying competition from developing countries shocked many traditional-minded executives from mainline firms into devising fresh strategies to respond to prices that often ranged from 30% to 40% below prevailing market pricing.

- Changing market behaviour, along with new flexible manufacturing techniques, convinced even the most sceptical executives about the vast opportunities and competitive advantages of creating specialized products and services targeted to dissimilar groups based on age, income, education, occupation, race, ethnic and cultural characteristics.

- Shifting life styles influenced marketers to focus on how different groups live, spend and act – all of which were being highlighted by the media and influenced by diverse political, economic, cultural, and social movements.

- Shortening product life cycles due to the proliferation of new products and the continuing flow of dazzling new and affordable technologies convinced executives to probe for emerging or previously unserved market segments. In turn, those circumstances triggered even greater efforts to push for faster-cheaper-smaller-better products.

- Continuing pressures on profitability and productivity activated the pervasive movement toward downsizing, re-engineering, and outsourcing. The result: a rush by many forward-looking executives to create market-sensitive organizations committed to total customer satisfaction.

Also, towards the end of the 20th Century, a powerful global frame-work emerged. Based on escalating technology, advances in computer-aided manufacturing techniques, low-cost skilled labour from Pacific Rim and Eastern Europe countries, skyrocketing progress in Internet commerce, substantial financial investments, and widespread industry alliances, cross-ocean titans such as DaimlerChrysler, BP Amoco and Bertelsmann-America Online came on the scene.

These new high-powered global firms, along with the other global giants, such as Procter & Gamble and Coca-Cola, began setting the pace on how marketing strategy would be practised in the new millennium. And not only by large conglomerates but by small and mid-size organizations, as well.

An outstanding example of best practices in marketing strategies for a new millennium organization is illustrated in the following case study.

Cisco Systems Inc.

The developer of technology networks, epitomizes how a marketing-driven company organizes for results, responds quickly to changes in market behaviour, and creates marketing strategies that relate to individual customer's needs. Labelled an outside-in (market-oriented) rather than an inside-out (production-oriented) organization, the San Jose, California company operates as a flexible, adaptive, customer-driven champion in its industry.

Founded in 1984 by a group of Stanford University (California) scientists, Cisco has mushroomed to annual revenues in excess of $28 billion. Behind such brilliant success are the underpinnings of how marketing strategy should be performed – by all organizations.

The central ideas behind those practices include:

- **Focus on the customer**. The ability to translate the outside-in approach into reality means permitting your core customers to decide your strategy. The essential concept is that they know more about what they need than your senior executives do.

- **Build networks**. The new information technology allows links among customers, suppliers, business partners, and employees. As a result, the continuous multi-directional flow of information and all the internal and external activities move in harmony from product concept to delivery of a wanted product to a customer. In turn, all these activities are encased

9

with superior service that resolves problems quickly and efficiently. Effectively applied, informational technology performs as a powerful competitive marketing strategy and effective business model that allows you to be far more virtual with customers and suppliers.

- **Create alliances**. In the current scheme of organizational and marketing strategy, alliances and other forms of partnering are keys to success. To make the connections work, Cisco maintains a seamless network of links by breeding a high level of trust among various managerial levels to achieve mutually agreed upon short and long-term goals.

- **Develop a corporate culture**. Indispensable to Cisco's organization is acquiring and maintaining a mind-set and an orientation that is totally customer-driven. A company's culture – expressed as values, things, ideas, and behavioural patterns – emerges to form healthy relationships, not only with customers and suppliers, but also with an attitude about employees as intellectual assets.

- **Apply technology**. Using the Internet as an integral part of the marketing strategy impacts directly on the traditional functions of the salesforce and customer service. For instance, Cisco obtains more than 50% of its revenues selling complex, expensive equipment over the Internet. Further, 7 out of 10 customer requests for technical support are filled electronically – at satisfaction rates that exceed face-to-face contact.

Summing up Cisco's strategy: Chief executive John T. Chambers believes the new rules of competition demand that organizations are:

1. Built on change, not stability.

2. Organized around networks, not a rigid hierarchy.

3. Based on interdependencies of partners, not self-sufficiency.

4. Constructed on technological advantage, not old-fashioned bricks and mortar.

Working with those guidelines, Chambers practises what he preaches by spending as much as 55% of his time with customers.

Combining marketing strategy with new technology

Picking up on Cisco's practices: The driving force behind the new applications of marketing strategy is your ability to harness information and technology into a powerful competitive weapon. And central to that strategy is the explosive use of the Internet. The Internet model – with fewer capital assets, a direct-to-customer connection, and freedom from the formal management structure – offers a significant level of speed and operational efficiency that is unsurpassed in its ability to foster exceptional levels of customer relationship marketing.

'I don't think there's been anything more important or more widespread in all my years at GE,' declared former General Electric Chairman Jack Welch. 'Where does the Internet rank in priority? It's number 1, 2, 3, and 4.'

Marketing successes

What effect has this new strategy model had in the competitive marketplace? Companies of all stripes have skyrocketed in their respective industries.

For example:

- Dell and Gateway continue to rely on sales of computers and an expanding line of other electronic products generated from direct-response marketing and the use of the Internet.

- Priceline.com, Orbitz.com, and Hotels.com have transformed the travel industry by allowing customers to plan itineraries and arrange online purchases of airline tickets, hotel rooms, and rental cars.

- Amazon.com started out selling books at a discount. Now it sells new and used books at up to 50% off the cover price. With competitors attempting to copy its every move, the company has diversified into toys, music, clothing, consumer electronics, food, household products, health and beauty items, tools, and sports equipment.

- Charles Schwab & Co. pioneered electronic trading and outperformed the traditional industry leaders in grabbing market share with its on-line brokerage services.

The following case shows how one organization grew from meagre beginnings to become a global powerhouse by making technology the centrepiece of its growth strategy.

Infosys Technologies Limited

Infosys began modestly as a computer services company in 1981, short on money and operating from one of the founder's bedrooms. Its first big break came when an Indian-based subsidiary of Germany's Bosch Group hired Infosys to run its data centre.

Slowly Infosys spread the word of its expertise to some of the biggest U.S. companies – including General Electric – by promising to provide quality services with cost savings of 50%. It was at this juncture that Infosys latched on to the leading edge of a rapidly expanding trend: Western companies began outsourcing a variety of low-tech and high-tech work to off-shore locations such as India and China.

For Infosys, the trend catapulted the company into the big leagues. The outsourcing movement triggered a profound change in how companies compete in a global competitive environment. So dramatic was the change that it reshaped Western business models, all to the advantage of Infosys and its direct competitors, Tata Consultancy Services and Wipro.

Infosys' strategies

Even as Infosys experienced high-level growth and a rising number of worldwide customers wanting to outsource their white-collar jobs, Infosys began facing the inevitable competition from its rivals, as well as from an increasing group of start-up companies. The pressure mounted for Infosys to maintain a market advantage and avoid getting entangled in predictable profit-draining price wars.

Faced with the problems of maintaining its momentum, Infosys did the following:

1. Instead of competing on costs, Infosys persuaded its Western customers to send more sophisticated work. As a result, Infosys' business-processing-outsourcing unit, which includes call centres and other routine activities, represents only 4.5% of its revenue.

2. A substantial 500-person research and development department was set up in Bangalore. Not only does the staff work directly on customers' problems, it also takes the initiative and develops new technology on its own. For instance, researchers

designed software that permits online banking with any hand-held computer and cellphone. In 2005, the company applied for 58 U.S. patents.

3. To sustain its market advantage, Infosys is firmly dedicated to developing and maintaining a highly-skilled workforce. To that end the company recruits experienced workers who can perform a variety of high-tech functions, such as writing sophisticated software programs, designing airplane components, processing mortgage applications, and maintaining computer systems for its large multinational customers. Also, the company actively recruits recent college graduates and puts them through an intensive training regimen that shapes them into high-performing 'Infoicons.'

What can you learn from the Infosys case? The following principles emerge:

Trends

Look for trends that complement your organization's existing competencies and permit aligning the company with emerging movements.(However, be certain those changes are consistent with the overall strategic objectives of your organization and that they fit correctly with the culture of the organization.) Fortuitously, Infosys latched on to an outsourcing trend. Then, when competition started to heat up, it exploited the situation by embedding technical personnel with customers and siphoning off the more challenging, higher-margin work assignments. Germane to achieving that end, Infosys' staff took the initiative and funded technology solutions that its customers could not, or chose not to, handle on its own.

Competitive encounters

Avoid direct encounters that would deteriorate into competitive in-fighting, price wars, and the like. Infosys' strategy was to go upscale, which allowed for more manoeuverability to deliver innovative products and high-value services. Therein lies the counter-measure to falling into the commodity trap that often ends with damaging price wars.

Market position

Establish a unique market position that fortifies the image you want your company, products, and services to project over the long-term. Even if you enjoy a technology advantage, your competitive position is only as secure as the quality of your skilled and continually trained personnel who are motivated by effective leadership. Infosys invested heavily in making sure its personnel received ongoing training and were oriented to providing superior high-end services in areas such as consulting, computer-aided engineering, and R&D. Management was also continually aware that a vibrant corporate culture was the bedrock requirement for making sure that its market position and marketing strategies were aligned.

Marketing strategy

An historical panorama

It is now appropriate to survey the historical roots that activated the drive to new marketing strategies and spurred to prominence numerous start-up companies, which have become the cutting edge giants of today.

Looking at how marketing planning and strategy evolved over the decades can assist you in determining where your organization sits on the growth curve leading to 21st century success.

The 1950s

As Europe and Asia began rebuilding after the devastation of World War II, the 1950s became a period of overwhelming economic influence by the United States throughout most of the world. During that time, corporate planning dominated most of the larger U.S. companies.

Consisting primarily of production plans, this type of planning focused on satisfying an insatiable demand for consumer goods within the U.S., and with supplying industrial products to help those European and Asian countries ravaged by war rebuild their economies and redevelop consumer markets.

At the highest organizational levels, ranking officers developed corporate plans, while maintaining a dominant financial focus. Rarely did lower echelon managers participate in strategy planning sessions.

In contrast, lower level managers geared their planning to maximize productivity for the short-term satisfaction of market demand. Marketing as a distinct unifying function enveloping product development, marketing research, advertising, sales promotion, and field-selling did not exist at that time.

The 1960s

Strong consumer demand for products characterized the 1960s. The business environment was marked by intensified economic growth in most of the industrialized countries. Yet serious competition still remained limited. There was no urgency to change procedures, other than to keep the production lines moving efficiently. In general, what was produced was consumed.

In addition to developing markets in European industrialized countries, Third World countries slowly emerged as customers for products to sustain the basic needs of life. Such products included simple machines, some types of agricultural equipment, and basic transportation in the form of buses and bicycles.

Organizations began to look to business planning as a way to involve senior executives who represented such core activities as manufacturing, research and development, sales, and distribution. As part of a longer-term strategy, there was a conscious effort to integrate diverse business functions through a coordinated plan of operations. In spite of this planning breakthrough, however, long-term plans were still kept separate from those short-term plans prepared by middle managers.

The 1970s

This decade triggered a transitional phase in planning and strategy. With the post-war rebuilding process about complete, its full effect was about to impact the world. European companies burst onto global markets. It was the Japanese companies, however, that generated the most aggressive and penetrating competition.

The full thrust of their competitive assault hit virtually every major industry from machine tools and consumer electronics to automobiles and steel. The new competitive situation ignited the surging movement to embrace marketing planning and competitive strategy.

In turn, marketing strategy during the 1970s signaled a period of market identification and expansion. In North America, customers demanded more varied products and services, and they were willing to pay for them. Responding to the continuing population shift out of the cities, businesses followed increasingly affluent customers into the expanding suburban shopping malls. In Western Europe and Asia new markets continued to unfold, thereby increasing consumption of consumer and industrial products.

Executives reshaped their organizations and merged the individual plans of the once scattered activities of merchandizing, advertising, sales promotion, publicity, and field-selling into a unified strategy to identify and satisfy changing market demands. Typically, the marketing plans developed by middle managers covered only a one-year period.

Within those plans, managers emphasized emerging geographic markets, new technology applications, and international markets. They made extensive use of demographic profiles to define markets with greater precision. Beyond demographics, a new approach to market definition emerged that utilized psychographics, a profiling system that described prospects by life style and behaviour.

Marketing as an independent business discipline expanded rapidly into undergraduate and graduate degree programs at universities worldwide. In keeping with the evolving and changing market conditions, a broad definition of marketing developed:

> *Marketing is a total system of interacting business activities designed to plan, price, promote, and distribute want-satisfying products or services to organizational and household users in a competitive environment at a profit.*

That definition emphasized understanding customer needs and developing comprehensive programs to satisfy the wants of different market segments. Further, a total system of interacting business activities called for integrating various business activities, such as manufacturing, research and development, promotion, and distribution. In turn, the definition also called for the use of strategy teams consisting of individuals from each of those diverse functions. It reaffirmed the integration already begun through business planning.

Managers viewed the marketing planning document as a 'housing' to contain all of the above functions and the resulting marketing strategies into a logical and organized format. To encourage clear and precise communications throughout the organization, the plan became the medium to reach all levels of the organization.

By the late 1970s, still another form of planning took hold: Strategic planning. Strategic planning aimed to build on to the long-term, financially-oriented corporate plans of the 1960s by adding a strategic focus to the process. More precisely:

> *Strategic planning is the managerial process of developing and maintaining a strategic fit between the organization and its changing market opportunities. It relies on developing:*
>
> - *a mission or strategic direction*
> - *objectives and goals*
> - *growth strategies*
> - *a business portfolio consisting of markets and products.*

Corporations still use the generalized terms strategic planning, corporate planning, and business planning and managers consider them part of a common business vocabulary. Regardless of the term used, the intent shows that volatile environmental, economic, industry, customer, and competitive factors require a more expansive and disciplined strategic thought process for effective planning and strategy development.

No longer could top-down 1950s-style corporate planning driven by a production orientation suffice. The evolving competitive global marketplace of the 1970s required a more precise orientation satisfied by strategic planning and marketing planning. In turn, that approach served as a springboard to the next level of planning.

The 1980s

The 1980s spurred the next stage of planning – strategic marketing planning – which merged two planning formats: the long-term strategic plan and the short-term marketing plan. (See Chapter 5 for details on developing a strategic marketing plan.)

There are several reasons why the strategic marketing plan evolved to this stage of the planning cycle:

1. While strategic planning permitted managers to create a long-term vision of how the organization could grow, for the most part it lacked implementation. A survey conducted by Deloitte & Touche Consulting indicated that while 97% of the Fortune 500 companies wrote strategic plans, only 15% of that elite group of companies ever implemented anything that came out of the plan.

2. Marketing planning, in turn, incorporated only those activities associated with the marketing function into an action-oriented plan. The planning period, however, was usually confined to one year. No formal process linked the longer-term strategic plan that required an implementation phase to the shorter-term marketing plan that warranted a strategic vision.

3. Typically, each plan developed independently within the organization. No procedure unified planning efforts consistent with the marketing definition of, '…a total system of interacting activities designed to plan, price, promote, and distribute want-satisfying products to organizational and household users in a competitive environment'.

Under these exceptional conditions, the strategic marketing plan evolved to create a linkage of the strategic plan with the marketing plan. It connected the internal functions of the organization with the external and volatile changes of a competitive global environment. In turn, the plan became the storehouse for marketing strategies.

The 1990s

As corporations of the 1980s and 1990s re-engineered and downsized to create cost-effective, efficient, and lean organizations, a further innovation evolved. The middle-level manager was asked to develop a formal strategy plan for his or her product, service, or business unit.

Using the strategic marketing plan as a hands-on format, the manager could now conceptualize a product with a long-term strategic direction that focuses on future customer and market needs. He or she could project what changes would take place in a framework of industry, consumer, competitive, and environmental areas and how technologies would change business practices. In addition, new groundbreaking software could identify buyer patterns and interpret their implications, so that marketing strategies could be adjusted to maximize profitability.

The 2000s

Intensive global competition will intensify; China and India will continue to grow and become powerful economic influences on world markets; major strategic alliances as well as minor joint marketing initiatives will accelerate by large and mid-size organizations. From a managerial viewpoint, the effective application of competitive strategies will saturate executives' time and energy as they immerse themselves in initiating efficient operations and adopting new technology innovations. According to McKinsey research, "Most CEO's claimed that they wanted to spend about a third of their time on strategy. That's about 80-days in a typical working year."

Strategy teams

Organizing for success

As you prepare for the marketing and competitive challenges in a global environment, it is essential that you and your staff retain a total customer orientation, adopt the technologies and information processes that will give you a competitive advantage, and maintain a staff of motivated and trained individuals. Within that framework, it is also in your best interest to utilize a strategy team as the supporting structure for your organization. Such a team is not a temporary ad hoc committee but a permanent part of the organizational framework and applicable to all sizes and levels of organizations.

Strategy teams evolved in earnest during the 1980s among those forward-looking organizations that embraced the then new definition of marketing as a total system of interacting business activities designed to plan, price, promote, and distribute want-satisfying products to household and organizational users at a profit.

These cross-functional teams were represented by individuals from diverse parts of the organization such as: manufacturing, marketing, sales, finance, distribution, and R&D. Strategy teams had various designations such as: business management teams, product management teams, and industry management teams. Each was centred on a particular segment of the market.

Generally, all teams had a common set of duties and responsibilities:

Duties

The strategy team serves as a significant contributor to the strategic marketing planning and strategy process with leadership roles in:

- Defining the business or product strategic direction.

- Analyzing the environmental, industry, customer, and competitor situations.

- Developing long and short-term objectives and strategies.

- Defining product, market, distribution, and quality plans to implement competitive strategies.

Responsibilities

- Create and recommend new or additional products.

- Approve all product and service modifications of a major nature.

- Act as a formal communications channel from the home office to the field.

- Plan and implement strategies throughout the product life cycle.

- Develop action plans to enhance a market position.

- Identify market trends and create opportunities in light of changing consumer demands.

- Coordinate efforts with various functions to achieve short and long-term objectives.

- Coordinate efforts for the exchange of new market or product opportunities among various functions, such as sales, manufacturing, product development, distribution, and finance.

- Develop a strategic marketing plan.

Identifying opportunities

A systematic approach

You should be able to create a team and prepare it with the overall duties and responsibilities described above. More specifically, the team should actively look for business-building opportunities to create action.

Use the following systematic approach to search for fresh market opportunities:

Opportunity 1

Search for opportunities in unserved, poorly served, or emerging market segments.

Actions:

- pursue new product or market niches;
- stretch product lines;
- position products to the needs of customers and against competitors.

Opportunity 2

Identify ways to create new opportunities.

Actions:

- differentiate and add value to products and services;
- participate in new technology, innovations, and manufacturing;
- pioneer something new or unique.

Opportunity 3

Look for opportunities through marketing creativity.

Actions:

- promote image through quality, performance, and training;
- use creativity in sales promotion, advertising, personal selling, and the Internet.

Opportunity 4

Monitor changing behavioural patterns and preferences.

Actions:

- practise segmenting markets according to behavioural patterns, demographic, and geographic information;
- identify clusters of customers who might buy or utilize different services for different reasons.

Opportunity 5
Learn from competitors and adapt strategies from other industries.

Action: Understand from your competitors:

- how they conduct business;
- what products they sell;
- what strategies they pursue;
- how they manufacture, distribute, promote, and price;
- their weaknesses, limitations, and possible vulnerabilities.

Best practices

Within most types of market-driven organizations, executives will have to face up to global competition, relationship marketing, and the fast-moving applications of informational technology. Common to all these issues is the use of marketing strategy as the all-encompassing action component.

Mastering the ingredients for marketing strategy includes the following:

1. Focus on the customer
Above all, customers are the focal point around which all parts of your product/service, promotion, pricing, and supply-chain activities must converge. The essential point: Customers know more about what they need than your executives do.

2. Build networks
Use information technology to link customers, suppliers, business partners, and employees. By encouraging a continuous flow of information, you will engage in ongoing communications from product concept to delivery of a wanted product to a customer. Effectively applied, informational technology performs as a powerful competitive marketing strategy and effective business model. It allows you to be far more virtual with customers and suppliers.

3. Create alliances
Acquisitions, alliances, and other forms of partnering are keys to success. To make the alliances work, however, requires a high level of trust and willingness to achieve mutually agreed upon, short and long-term goals.

4. Look at corporate culture

Understanding your organization's core values, maintaining an outside-in mind-set, and adopting an orientation that is totally customer-driven are central components of marketing strategy. Your company's culture – expressed as values, ideas, and behavioural patterns – should materialize to form healthy relationships with customers, suppliers, and employees.

5. Apply technology

The Internet is an integral part of most marketing strategies with immense impact on how the salesforce and customer service personnel can perform effectively.

6. Define a market position

Establish a distinctive market position that doesn't create confusion or misinterpretation, so that a competitor is not mistakenly identified with your position. Do so by selecting a position that conforms to your firm's unique, core competencies, so that competitors cannot easily duplicate the differentiating factors for which you can claim superiority. Also, communicate your position in precise terms through product applications, sales promotion, and advertising.

For example, determine what constitutes your position. Do you position your product with a single benefit, such as lowest cost; do you use a double benefit position of lowest cost and best technical support; or do you select a multi-benefit position of lowest cost, best technical support, and state-of-the-art technology?

These benefit positions, in turn, lay the foundation for developing the tactical programs that incorporate the marketing mix: product, price, promotion, and distribution.

Summary

The new rules of competition demand organizations built on change, organized around networks, based on interdependencies of partners, and constructed on technological advantage.

2

How to manage your marketing strategy (Part 1)

Chapter objectives

Primary strategy principles

Strategy applications

A focus on marketing strategy

Best practices

Chapter objectives

After reading this chapter, you should be able to:

1. Outline the historical roots of strategy and relate them to modern marketing practice.

2. Identify the marketing principles that have originated from classic military strategy and apply them to your short and long-term business plans.

3. Employ the five primary strategy applications of speed, indirect approach, concentration, alternative objectives, and unbalancing competition to achieve a competitive advantage.

Since the time the ancient Greeks coined the word strategia (or strategos), meaning to lead an army or generalship, thousands of generals have used military strategy to conquer territories and gain power. To impose their wills on others, they had to distract and unbalance their opponents physically and psychologically. Faced with a conflict of wills, the generals on the battlefield were forced to maximize the effectiveness of their economic and human resources to achieve their goals.

These military challenges, outwitting competing wills, gaining territory and power, and conserving resources while expanding influence, are precisely those of business. Thus, the long history of documented military strategies of attack and defence provide an excellent resource for businesses.

Most confrontations – whether military, business, or even athletic – involve a defence protecting its ground and an offence trying to overtake that ground. The key to offensive strategy is the efficient use of resources to accomplish the attack and overtake the territory – or market segment.

The military perspective provides five primary strategy principles that can strengthen your comprehension of strategy, along with their further application for meeting most competitive challenges. These principles include direct attack, indirect attack, envelopment attack, bypass attack, and guerrilla attack.

Primary strategy principles

Direct attack

A direct attack in many business situations results in exhausting budgets and people. That translates into using the salesforce, advertising, distribution, manufacturing, and other company resources without achieving the desired objectives.

Even if a company does accomplish some minor objective, such as minimal sales or a nominal share of market, few or no resources would remain for penetrating the market and realizing its full potential. Using the military equivalent: No resources remain to 'get off the beaches' before the counter-attack succeeds in getting pushed back 'into the sea'.

Support for the above assertions comes from one of the most respected military historians of the 20th century, Basil Liddell Hart. In his book *Strategy*, the British author presents a massive study covering 12 wars that decisively affected the entire course of European history in ancient times and 18 major wars of modern history up to 1914. In all, these 30 conflicts embraced more than 280 major military campaigns, and spanned 2,500 years.

The study reveals that in only six of these campaigns did a decisive result follow a direct frontal attack. And of those six most began with an indirect attack but were changed to a direct attack due to a variety of battlefield conditions.

Consequently, Liddell Hart states:

> 'History shows that rather than resign himself to a direct approach a great captain will take even the most hazardous indirect approach – if necessary over mountains, deserts or swamps with only a fraction of his force even cutting loose from his communications. He prefers to face any unfavourable condition rather than accept the risk of frustration inherent in a direct approach.'

Thus, reviewing the overwhelming evidence of history, we can conclude the following:

1. No general is justified in launching his troops in a direct attack upon an enemy who is firmly in position.

2. In like manner, we can interchange the concept and assert with strong confidence that no manager is justified in launching sales and marketing forces in a direct campaign against a competitor who is entrenched in an actively defended market-leader position.

3. Consequently, if there is little or no differentiation in such areas as product, promotion, pricing, or distribution – as perceived by the market – there is minimal chance of success.

Just how much stronger is the defence against a direct attack? The military genius Napoleon estimated a three-to-one advantage was needed to break through a defender's line in a direct frontal attack. In Napoleon's time, a three-to-one advantage meant having three times more infantry, artillery, and cavalry – and employing three times more logistical support than was available to the defender. Therefore, even if a breakthrough did occur by using a massive infusion of resources, inadequate human and material resources would remain for follow-up and penetration.

In business terms, a three-to-one advantage translates into three times more salespeople, advertising expenditures, logistical, and administrative support – a huge expenditure of resources for little, or perhaps, no return.

A classic business example of a direct attack occurred when General Electric, RCA, and Xerox launched a direct frontal attack during the 1970s against the formidable IBM, an entrenched defender of its computer market. These companies attempted to penetrate IBM's active defenses with an undifferentiated product. Those companies lost millions on the venture and retreated from that market.

To add still another perspective to the negatives of the direct attack: During World War II, the renowned General Douglas MacArthur stated at a strategy meeting with U.S. President Franklin D. Roosevelt, 'The use of a direct frontal attack is a sign of a mediocre commander and there is no room in modern warfare for such a commander'.

To paraphrase MacArthur for our topic:

The use of a direct frontal attack against an entrenched competitor is a sign of a mediocre manager and there is no room in today's competitive environment for such a manager!

Indirect attack

If the direct attack puts the active defender at an advantage; if it requires the aggressor to expend an enormous quantity of resources, thereby depriving it of strength for market penetration, and where such an attack would likely result in failure, then an alternative approach must do the opposite. To place the defender at a disadvantage, it is necessary to concentrate on its weaknesses. At the same time, an effective strategy should channel the attacker's resources to maximizing market share, rather than exhausting them in the attack.

According to Liddell Hart, the indirect attack is the most fruitful approach. It has the greatest chance of success while conserving the greatest amount of strength.

Application

When an indirect attack is applied as a business strategy, the attacker concentrates on a weakness in those market segments that are emerging, neglected, or poorly served by competitors. Such a segment is the initial point of entry.

What follows the entry is the selection of a strategy using the marketing mix as a resource. Refer to the following chapter, Figure 3.1 Creating strategies out of the marketing mix, for a complete list of strategy possibilities.

Strategies could be in a product, in price (a computer cheap enough for students to afford), in promotion (mineral water targeted at upper-class consumers), or in distribution (DVDs dispensed at commuter train stations).

Once entrenched in the initial market segment, thereby establishing a market presence with a customer base, suppliers, and a supply chain network, the attacker can more easily secure parts of the market previously dominated by competitors. This critical follow-up to entry is called market expansion.

Examples abound of the advantages of the indirect attack in business:

- German and Japanese car makers first entered the North American automobile market with small cars, a market essentially neglected by domestic manufacturers during the 1970s and poorly served during the 1980s.

- Miller discovered the light beer segment as an emerging market.

- Honeywell for years concentrated its computers at the medium and small-size cities initially unattended by IBM.

- Apple became a dominant factor in schools early on, specifically serving that segment with computer hardware and software, also left vacant by IBM.

- Wal-Mart originally opened its stores in towns with populations under 2,500, ignored at that time by the leading retailers.

With the abundance of business examples and with evidence from military history, there is never any justification for a manager to undertake a direct frontal attack in today's competitive market. Rather, it is a manager's obligation and necessity to use an indirect approach to:

1. Find an unattended, poorly served, or emerging market segment.

2. Create a competitive advantage by using the marketing mix (product, price, promotion, and distribution) in a configuration that cannot be easily matched by competitors. That means applying your maximum strength against the weaknesses of your opponent.

3. Mobilize all available resources on fulfiling the unmet needs and wants of the selected market in a strength-conserving manner. Then work diligently at solidifying relationships with your customers for the long-term.

4. Expand into additional segments of the market in a planned, deliberate approach that keeps in mind the overwhelming advantages of the indirect approach.

Envelopment attack

An envelopment strategy consists of two stages:

- First, beginning as an indirect attack, the attacker focuses on a specific market segment for a point of entry.

- Second, by identifying additional market segments and adding new products, the attacker then uses an expansion strategy to envelop the entire market.

In the consumer market, Seiko illustrates the indirect-envelopment combination. The Japanese company initially entered the watch market in one segment, digital watches, and then enveloped the overall market by offering as many as 400 models of watches to penetrate every major watch outlet and customer segment – and generally overwhelmed their competitors.

In the industrial sector, The Timken Company offers 26,000 shaped ballbearing combinations, a product line unmatched by any competitor. The company thereby enveloped that market segment and fulfilled practically all its customers' needs in that product category.

Bypass attack

The bypass attack allows the attacker to circumvent its chief competitors and diversify into unrelated products or unrelated geographical markets for existing products.

For example, Eastman Kodak Co. successfully used a bypass approach into such diverse areas as electronics and biotechnology, with products as diverse as electronic publishing systems, cattle feed nutrients, and anti-cancer drugs.

However, this relatively sudden move into diverse fields followed an ultraconservative period in which Kodak temporarily stalled and competitors grabbed such markets as instant photography, 35mm cameras, and video recorders. All of which were natural extensions of Kodak's core business. The bypass strategy does include a measure of risk because expansion into a range of unrelated fields can diminish a company's strength in any single area.

An example of a somewhat unsuccessful use of bypass strategy is the Colgate-Palmolive Company. Although Colgate surpassed the Procter & Gamble Co. in many European markets and maintained a lead for its existing products there, in most North American markets Colgate remained behind Procter & Gamble.

Guerrilla attack

Guerrilla attack involves small intermittent attacks on different markets. It is useful for a small company competing against a large corporation, or where a product with a small market share is combating a brand leader. It can also be executed by a larger organization against its competitors.

Guerrilla attacks are characterized by a number of actions: selective price cuts, supply interference, executive raids, intensive promotional bursts, and assorted legal actions. The aim is movement and surprise to create confusion and distraction, and to cause the opposing manager to make mistakes.

Strategy applications

With the discussion of attack techniques in mind, we can now bridge the vast historical perspective of military strategy with the more recent view of business. The military-marketing connection can be summed up in the following perceptive and parallel statements:

'The object of war is a better state of peace.'

B. H. LIDDELL HART

'The object of business is to create a customer.'

PETER DRUCKER

From the 2,500 years of recorded military history we find five ruling applications that are characteristic of all well executed strategies – practical principles that you can use in your business to develop successful competitive strategies.

These applications consist of speed, indirect approach, concentration, alternative objectives, and unbalancing competition. A thorough understanding of these practical guidelines is critical for you to implement business-building strategies.

Below you will find descriptions of the strategy guidelines, examples from actual corporations, and step-by-step procedures for applying them to your firm.

Speed

Speed is an essential ingredient in the effective application of marketing strategy. There are few cases of overlong, dragged-out campaigns that have been successful. Exhaustion – the draining of resources – has killed more companies than almost any other factor.

Extended deliberation, procrastination, cumbersome committees, and long chains of command from home office to the field are all detriments to success.

Drawn out efforts often divert interest, diminish enthusiasm, and depress morale. Individuals become bored and their skills lose sharpness. The gaps of time created through lack of action give competitors a greater chance to react and blunt your efforts.

In today's competitive business environment it is in your best interest to evaluate, manoeuvre, and concentrate your marketing forces quickly to gain the most profit at least cost in the shortest span of time. In one case, IBM acted quickly to invade Japanese markets, while bringing legal action against its Japanese competitor for illegally obtaining IBM's operating codes.

In another situation, Heublein, makers of Smirnoff vodka, moved rapidly to reposition its product and introduce two new brands to envelop three market segments before Seagram could respond with an adequate strategy for its brand of Wolfschmidt vodka.

The proverbs 'Opportunities are fleeting' or 'The window of opportunity is open' have an intensified truth in today's markets. Speed is essential for gaining the advantage and exploiting the advantage gained.

Organizing for speed and quick reaction

Two factors make it possible for the manager to react with speed:

1. New technologies in product development, communications, and computerization challenge companies to set up organizations to react quickly and decisively in a ratio of a short span of time to a large amount of space.

2. Even with new technology, gathering market intelligence entails long periods of research, experiment, and investment for each marketing situation. Therefore, for maximum speed the essential ingredient is an efficient organization that simplifies the system of control and, in particular, shortens the chain of command.

Your own experience may well support the obvious conclusion that an organization with many levels in its decision-making process cannot operate with speed. This situation exists because each link in a chain of command carries four drawbacks:

1. Loss of time in getting information back.

2. Loss of time in sending orders forward.

3. Reduction of the top executive's full knowledge of the situation.

4. Decrease in the top executive's personal influence on managers.

Therefore, to make your marketing effort effective, reduce the chain of command. The fewer the intermediate levels, the more dynamic the operations tend to become. The result is improved effectiveness of the total marketing effort and increased flexibility.

A more flexible organization can achieve greater market penetration because it has the capacity to adjust to varying market circumstances, support alternative objectives, and concentrate at the decisive points. Organizational flexibility is further enhanced by setting up cross-functional strategy teams consisting of junior and middle managers, representing different functional areas of the organization. (See Chapter 1 for a listing of duties and responsibilities of a strategy team.)

Application

To increase the speed of your operations and improve your flexibility, follow these guidelines:

1. Reduce the chain of command in your company and increase the pace of communications from the field to the home office.

2. Bring into play junior managers for their ideas, flexibility, and initiatives for identifying and taking advantage of new opportunities.

3. Use a cross-functional strategy team to tap areas of cultural diversity that may exist in your firm, thereby permitting you to benefit from multiple perspectives.

Indirect approach

As already noted in the discussion of military strategy, you should avoid the frontal attack at all costs in favour of an indirect approach, which can include any of the non-direct forms of attack: envelopment, bypass, or guerrilla.

The object of the indirect approach is to circumvent the strong points of resistance and concentrate in the markets of opportunity with a competitive advantage built around product, price, promotion, and distribution.

A familiar example is Japanese copier makers attacking Xerox by initially avoiding the big copier market where Xerox had dominance, and concentrating instead on the vacant small copier segment. Also, as noted earlier, German and Japanese firms dominating the small car market in North America further illustrates an indirect attack centred on market segmentation and product positioning that avoids a direct confrontation.

Other cases have become marketing legends:

*   Columbia House used an indirect approach centred on distribution to start the first record club.

*   Book-of-the-Month Club started in the late 1920s and circumvented the traditional bookstore as the 'only' way to sell books.

- Sony Corp. entered the North American and European markets with a small TV in the early 1970s, thereby using the indirect approach against the inbred giants that focused only on larger sets.

- Amazon.com has become a legend in its own time by using the Internet, and a vast selection of discounted book titles, as an indirect approach to outflank most other book sellers and cause still others to scramble to catch up.

Concentration

Concentration has two uses in strategy terms:

1. It means directing your resources toward a market or group and fulfiling its specific needs and wants. In modern marketing practice, concentration applies to target marketing, segmentation, and niche marketing.

2. As applied to strategy, concentration means focusing your strengths against the weaknesses of your competitor.

How do you determine the weaknesses of the competitor? When developing your marketing strategy, conduct a competitive analysis (see Chapter 4, How to manage your competitor intelligence) to detect the strength-weakness relationship. From the analysis, you can then isolate the areas of competitive weakness and thereby determine where to apply your strength.

Application

To concentrate in a market, use as many of the following techniques as appropriate to your company's situation:

1. As with the indirect approach, use competitive analysis to identify your competitors' weaknesses and your company's strengths.

2. Concentrate on a market segment that you have determined represents growth and, in turn, could help launch you into additional market segments.

3. Introduce a differentiated product (or product modification) not already developed by existing competitors.

4. Develop multilevel distribution by private labelling of your product for existing suppliers. Concurrent with that action, establish your own brand. Therefore, if one strategy falters the alternative strategy often wins.

5. Follow-up by expanding into additional market segments with the appropriate products so you can envelop the entire market category, providing your firm has the resources to sustain the effort.

Alternative objectives

There are four central reasons for developing alternative, or multiple objectives:

1. On a corporate scale, most businesses have to fulfill several long and short-term goals and require various approaches for their attainment. Therefore, they need a wide range of objectives with a variety of time frames.

2. As already discussed, the strategy principle of concentration is implemented successfully only through the application of alternative objectives.

3. Alternative objectives permit enough flexibility to exploit opportunities as they arise. By designing a number of objectives, any of which can be used depending on circumstances, you hold options for achieving one objective when others fail.

4. Most important, alternative objectives keep your competitors on the 'horns of a dilemma' – unable to detect your real intentions. By displaying a number of possible threats, you force a competing manager to spread his resources and attention to match your action.

While you have dispersed intentionally in order to gain control, you cause him to disperse erratically, inconveniently, and without full knowledge of the situation. Thus, you cause the opposing manager to lose control. Then you can concentrate rapidly on the objective that offers the best potential for success.

Since the major incalculable is the human will (the mind of one manager against the mind of a competing manager), the intent of alternative objectives is to unbalance the opposing manager into making mistakes through inaction, distraction, wrong decisions, false moves, or misinterpretation of your real intent.

You thereby expose a weakness that you can exploit through concentration of effort. This unbalancing or dislocation is achieved through movement and surprise.

g

The above guidelines of strategy are summarized in the following examples:

- *Deere & Company* created a range of alternative market and product objectives by moving beyond its basic farm equipment business – while remaining true to its core competencies – by entering the consumer lawn-tractor market, manufacturing engine blocks and diesel engines, producing forestry and earthmoving equipment, and making chassis, for recreational vehicle manufacturers.

- *Reynolds Metals, a unit of Alcoa Inc.,* selected additional target segments beyond its stronghold in aluminium cans and building materials. It created indirect opportunities in consumer plastic packaging and created a thriving business, including: aluminium foil, wax paper and cooking bags, resealable food storage bags and wraps.

- *Maytag, a brand of Whirlpool Corp.,* shaped a concentration strategy on defending and attacking the medium-priced mass market and lower-end homebuilders' segments for its washing and drying machines. Maytag thereby maintained flexibility about which segment it would defend and where it would aggressively increase market share.

While the actions described may appear as simple moves for expansion or diversification, they actually serve as deliberate strategies to keep competitors guessing as to where the concentration will take place. The alternative objectives and strategies illustrated cut across a wide range of opportunities that send confusing signals to competitors, thereby permitting maximum flexibility in selecting areas for concentration.

Application

To use alternative objectives, follow these guidelines:

1. Consider such areas as customer service, improved delivery time, extended warranties, sales terms, after-sales support, packaging, and management training as sources of alternative objectives.

2. Identify alternative niches in the initial stages of attack to cause distraction among your competitors.

3. Exploit your competitors' confusion by concentrating your efforts on the weak spots that represent opportunities.

Unbalancing competition

Victory in many competitive situations is not necessarily due to the brilliance of the attacker or defender, but to the mistakes of the opposing manager. If brilliance plays a roll at all, it is in the manager's deliberate efforts to develop situations that unbalance the competition.

Those efforts, in turn, produce the psychological and physical unbalancing effects on the opposing manager through speed, indirect approach, concentration, and alternative objectives. Moreover, unbalancing fulfills strategy's ultimate purpose: the reduction of resistance.

You might try an unbalancing action, for example, by announcing a new product that could make the competing manager's product line obsolete. Even a press release about a yet-to-be released product line can 'make them sweat' and create panic – and mistakes. This unbalancing is practiced continuously in day-to-day activities that range from the threat of legal action to the effects of mergers and acquisitions.

Application

To unbalance competition, use these guidelines:

1. Identify the areas in which the competition is not able (or willing) to respond to your actions. (See Chapter 4, How to manage your competitor intelligence.)

2. Make a conscious effort to create an unbalancing effect through surprise announcements, for example, of a new computerized ordering procedure, just-in-time delivery, or technical on-site assistance. The unbalancing effect will have the greatest impact to the extent that you are able to maintain secrecy until the last possible moment.

3. Utilize new technology to unbalance competitors and make them rush to catch up. Investigate the various technologies applied to marketing, such as the Internet to speed technical and customer-service assistance from manufacturer to customer, and new applications of interactive video systems.

The following case example summarizes the concepts and techniques discussed so far.

SAS

This large software company is a leader in business intelligence software and services. Customers use SAS software to improve performance by providing greater insight into vast amounts of data, which results in faster and more accurate business decisions, more profitable relationships with customers and suppliers, and more frequent research breakthroughs. SAS managers have also succeeded in devising strategies fine-tuned to customers' problems, competitors' behaviours, industry transitions, and environmental changes.

For instance, over the past few years, management capitalized on customers' concerns over two major events: the new millennium and the euro with its widespread cross-border influences. Each would have generated monumental communications and internal operating problems among those customers using existing computer systems.

SAS's early insights into those customers' needs paid off in a big way. Rather than indulge in time-consuming tasks of fixing existing systems, a vast majority of its customers bought all-new software packages. The result: in one year SAS sales skyrocketed 63%.

But what does the company do for an encore?

SAS strategy

Energized by the swelling momentum, SAS managers were motivated to devise a fresh strategy to dominate the software market for the long-term. Note in the following list the creative application of the strategy principles described in this chapter.

SAS moved rapidly to:

- Refocus its business to adapt to the highly competitive market for its statistical software that tracks changes in the way customers buy and use its products. One system calls for linking suppliers and customers by using unique software to track an entire industrial process from its starting point. For example, raw material from South Africa moves to a car plant in France, then to a dealer showroom in Italy.

- Envelop the vast array of business-to-business markets and expand into a leadership position within the industries it serves. SAS broke its traditional policy of secrecy and revealed its proprietary codes to eager developers worldwide, so they could create specialized applications software on a market-by-market roll out. The object: rapid deployment of software packages to gain a jump on the giants such as Microsoft and Computer Associates.

- Concentrate on viable market niches. SAS moved to change its long-held practice by enlisting a network of resellers to distribute its software to mid-size and small businesses.

- Observe how smaller competitors may have stumbled in their product design or ability to market their offerings effectively. SAS moved rapidly to correct the errors, launched its product with precision into targeted niches, and pryed away market share from competitors.

Action strategies

From the SAS case and the principles cited in this chapter, four major strategy lessons stand out:

1. While the tools of marketing (advertising, sales promotion, field-selling, marketing research, distribution, pricing) are physical acts, they are directed by a mental process. The greater attention you pay to your customers, competitors, industry trends, and the environment the more easily you will gain the upper hand and the less it will cost.

2. The tougher you make your marketing practices, the more your competitors will consolidate against you. Result: You will harden the resistance you are trying to overcome. Even if you succeed in winning the market, you will have fewer resources with which to profit from the victory. Therefore, establish long-term bonding relationships with customers and suppliers; and work together to the profitable growth of your markets. To repeat the late Peter Drucker's maxim, 'The object of business is to create a customer.'

3. The more intent you are on securing a market entirely on your own terms, the stiffer the obstacles you will raise in your path. And the more cause competitors will have to try to reverse what you have achieved. Therefore, don't intentionally seek direct competitor confrontations, it will exhaust resources and divert your attention from your customers' needs and problems. Instead, use the indirect approach.

4. When you are trying to dislodge your competitor from a strong market position, leave that competitor a quick way to exit the market. Do so by increasing the gap between you and your competitor through product differentiation and value-added services.

A focus on marketing strategy

The five strategy applications – speed, indirect approach, concentration, alternative objectives, and unbalancing the competition – characterize the formation of marketing strategies. This section will now condense them into three fundamental components: indirect approach, differentiation, and concentration.

Understanding these principles will help you incorporate the strategy principles into a fine-turned actionable plan, and thereby help you devise marketing strategies to outperform competitors.

Indirect approach

As discussed in the earlier section of this chapter and demonstrated in the SAS example, avoid a direct approach against an entrenched competitor. The odds are totally against you. Instead, where possible, take some of the following actions:

- Create uncertainty in the minds of opposing managers as to your real intentions about specific areas such as time and place of product launch, pricing strategies, or promotion intensity.

- Search for unserved market segments and fill product gaps quickly. Do so in a way that pre-empts competitors and thereby permits you to gain a foothold in the target segment with little or no opposition.

- Gain access to the supply chain through add-on services or special inducements.

- If appropriate, use legal actions or other unorthodox approaches to dislodge a competitor.

In all actions use speed to create surprise, which in turn will cause confusion among your competitors. Then use alternative objectives to further reinforce the dilemma in your competitor's mind about your intentions.

Differentiation

The most effective means of applying the indirect approach is to seek differentiation in the areas of the marketing mix (product, price, promotion, and distribution). It is important to remember that even if your product may seem like an indistinguishable commodity, there are always ways to differentiate it.

Writes Harvard Professor Theodore Levitt: 'There is no such thing as a commodity.' His suggestions for differentiating products and services are summarized as follows:

- Consider differentiation in such tangible areas as customer service, improved delivery time, extended warranties, sales terms, after-sales support, packaging, and management training of your own staff and that of your distributors.

- Try differentiation with such intangibles as reliability, image, nice-to-do-business-with reputation, credibility, prestige, convenience, value, responsiveness to problems, and access to key individuals in your firm.

While the competitive products may be identical, the suggested areas of differentiation add up to a total product package that moves you away from the commodity status and gives you a competitive edge, with the added potential for premium pricing.

Concentration

Your ability to implement concentration is predicted on the effective applications of the indirect approach and differentiation. Concentration is successful to the degree that you can distract the competitor and seek out an opportunity in an unserved, emerging, or neglected segment. Concentration is also effective only to the extent that you can differentiate yourself from the competitor.

This particular component is so vital to successful strategies that Liddell Hart indicated that if all of strategy could be summed up into one word, it would be 'concentration'.

Competitor intelligence

You can apply these three fundamentals of strategy only if adequate competitive intelligence is used. For example, identifying emerging markets is useful to the extent that you can pre-empt your competition and satisfy the needs and wants of those markets.

Or, employing areas of differentiation is advantageous to the extent that the competitors cannot or are not willing to respond to your action. The confidence level of your strategy is strengthened by your diligent efforts in using competitor analysis to shape an indirect approach.

Best practices

For effective strategy development, use these guidelines for success:

Know your market
Pinpoint the critical strategic points for market entry. Initially look at geographic location, availability of distributors, and buying motives of the targeted buyers. What entry point would give you the best possibility to manoeuvre?

Assess competitors' intentions and strategies
Evaluate how energetically competitors will challenge your intrusion into their markets. Are they willing to forfeit a piece of the business to you as long as you don't become too aggressive?

Determine the level of technology required
While technology adeptness often wins many of today's markets, there are still numerous low-tech niche opportunities open to a smaller company. Where does your company fit on the technology issue?

Evaluate your internal capabilities and competencies
One of the cornerstones to manoeuvring in today's market is the ability to turn out a quality product equal to or better than your competitors. What are your company's outstanding competencies?

Maintain discipline and vision
Attempting to manoeuvre among market leaders takes confidence, courage, and know-how develop a winning strategy. How would you assess your company's willingness to challenge a market leader?

Secure financial resources
Upper-level management support is necessary to obtain the finances to sustain an ongoing activity. If competitors detect any weakness, they can easily play the waiting game for the financially unsteady organization to cave in. What type of support can you count on?

Develop a launch plan to market the product
Shape a marketing mix that incorporates a quality product, appropriate distribution, adequate promotion, and a market-oriented price to attract buyers. Which part of the mix would represent your driving force?

Maintain a keen awareness of how customers will respond to your product offering

Use market intelligence to gain insight about what motivates various groups to buy your product. What immediate action can you undertake to target a niche and avoid a head-on confrontation with a market leader?

3

How to manage your
marketing strategy (Part 2)

Chapter objectives

Part 1 – Marketing mix

Part 2 – External forces

Best practices

Chapter objectives

After reading this chapter, you should be able to:

1. Apply market-tested strategies to your own business.

2. Utilize the marketing mix as a resource for developing strategies and tactics.

3. Observe those external market forces that can make or break a business: customers, competitors, industry, and the environment.

4. Devise competitive marketing strategies to outperform your competitors.

'Marketing strategy is the most significant planning challenge regardless of industry or size of company. Our goal will be to re-evaluate and examine constantly our marketing position. Our emphasis will be on market strategy, technique, and product innovation.'

SOURCE: PRICEWATERHOUSECOOPERS' SURVEY OF CORPORATE EXECUTIVES

The survey pinpoints marketing strategy as the pivotal activity that should drive your actions, regardless of your industry and the size of your company. Given that dynamic trend, what are some identifiable characteristics of marketing strategies and how can you translate them into meaningful actions for your own business?

The following sampling of companies show the all-encompassing impact of strategies and how it infiltrates virtually every level of those organizations:

- **Umpqua Bank** is small compared to the likes of Citibank, Chase, and Sumitomo. The marketing question is how to stay viable and develop a strategy of differentiation to set it apart from the market leaders? Umpqua adopted a broad-based approach with experiential marketing, also known as the 'Starbucks Effect.' The technique draws in customers not only to buy the brand, but also to internalize a buying experience.

  When customers walk into the bank's branch location, they are just as likely to enjoy a cup of coffee as they are to make a deposit. The bank doesn't consider its locations branches. Rather, they are retail stores where people can lounge, surf the Web, listen to music, and browse literature on banking services in a relaxed atmosphere. To accomplish the transformation, employees undergo a customer-service training program produced by luxury hotel chain Ritz-Carlton. And some store managers are hired more for their retail background than their financial knowledge.

- **Endo Pharmaceuticals** found itself straddling a win/lose situation. Its flagship product is Lidoderm, a skin patch widely prescribed to relieve aches and pains. It has the dubious honour of representing two-thirds of Endo's revenues and three-quarters of its profits. The marketing problem is how do you deal with a single product and very little in the pipeline to replace Lidoderm should some unforeseen event cause sales to drop. An intermediate solution came from the marketplace. Managers noticed that physicians were prescribing Lidoderm for other than its original purpose of lessening pain caused by shingles. Doctors were recommending it for all sorts of other ailments, from lower back pain to tennis elbow, and plain old sore muscles. Digging deeper into product usage, managers also noticed that those 'other' applications represented more than half of Lidoderm prescriptions. Picking up on the highly useful usage trend, Endo management trained its sales reps to provide doctors with documented studies showing the effectiveness of Lidoderm in relieving pain from such additional ailments as diabetes and osteoarthritis. The strategy worked to extend the product's sales life. And forecasts show that Lidoderm will continue to make healthy sales growth.

- **Home Depot** continuously tests for improvements inside and outside its total operation. It's an ongoing competitive strategy to gain market share, increase same-store sales, and identify new segment opportunities. For instance, it keeps some stores open 24-hours a day and offers truck rentals to encourage shoppers to splurge on large high-priced products. The company even ranks distributors' performance to determine those that qualify for added support and still others that should be retrained or even discharged. Results: Store sales skyrocketed 9% in one quarter alone and overall earnings jumped 39% in one year.

- **Capital One Financial**, issuer of credit cards, uses rigorous consumer research to identify viable customer segments and fine-tune its new products. It thereby reduces the risk of loss and improves the chance of success long before an actual product launch.

- **Cadbury** runs a sweepstake using codes on candy wrappers. To find out who won, a prospect using a cellular phone text messages the code to a designated number. The strategy makes use of mobile marketing. While still in the early-stages of a marketing/sales cycle, the pervasive use of the mobile (cell) phone is attracting innovative applications.

For example: In Sweden, if an individual wants to park in an open, designated spot, it can be reserved via a mobile phone for a certain time period. Throughout Europe, individuals who want to log their opinions or get coupons, can do it through a mobile phone. As a fully-fledged and ever-present communications channel, the mobile phone, as with the Internet, has to be made part of the marketing mix strategy.

- **Dell Computer** didn't wait for its product lines to mature. Managers quickly recognized changes in market needs and translated its much-touted manufacturing flexibility into meeting and satisfying new market trends. For example, Dell shifted into new products swiftly to meet the frenzied pace of new PC opportunities, such as the growing under $1,000 segment.

  Further, Dell's manufacturing flexibility translated to its remarkably efficient internal communications flow through which orders rush from the Internet or telephone salesperson directly to the factory floor, where customized computers are built and shipped in a matter of hours.

- **Gap Inc.** focuses sharply on its superior customer service, swift manufacturing capabilities, and combines them with a total customer orientation. Those attributes spill over to the design of stylish fashions to suit selected markets defined by demographic, cultural, and geographic characteristics.

Underscoring the above examples are two central issues that must be addressed regardless of business or industry: market and organization.

1. Market

This issue relates to your company's capabilities to satisfy the specific needs and solve the unique problems of selected groups in your target segments. And you do so in a competitive environment by developing workable alliances with suppliers, even where your competitor may be a supplier. (See the following case study.)

2. Organization

This issue probes your managerial ability to coordinate with virtually every function of your company and to do so with the expectations that you can satisfy the varied demands of diverse market segments better than your competitors. That is accomplished by fully internalizing the belief that effective strategies can flow from just about any part of the organization – as illustrated by the above examples.

The following case study further illustrates these issues.

Lenovo Group Ltd

China's leading PC maker has moved from a fledgling money-losing organization, originally known as the Legend Group, to the premier market leader in China today. Lenovo enjoys a dominant 35% market share in China and ranks as the world's third-largest PC company with 4.7% market share. However, it was the purchase of IBM's PC operations in 2005 that created the quantum leap into the big leagues and made revenues skyrocket to $13 billion in revenues.

Lenovo's strategic plans call for achieving dual objectives:

1. Expand to other emerging markets and make Lenovo into a high-profile global brand.

2. Increase its already dominant market share in China – a market that now holds the singular honor as the world's fastest-growing computer market.

What is behind the marketing strategy that gives rise to such dazzling performance against powerful foreign competitors, most of whom enjoy international brand recognition? Let's examine the key strategies structured around product, price, promotion, and distribution:

Product

With the help and advice of its suppliers, primarily IBM, Lenovo eliminated its once shabby image of producing a low quality product. It shifted resolutely to developing state-of-the-art, powerful PCs while honing an image as a high-tech dynamo. Placing its efforts where its goals are, Lenovo dedicates a hefty 20% of its R&D budget to come up with cutting-edge product ideas. Where the previous policy was to squeeze every penny out of costs, the strategy now is to ask, "What new ideas do we have?"

Lenovo anchors its efforts to a two-pronged strategy that first looks outward and uses its enhanced products to meet the needs of a huge and growing market. Second, it works backwards and strengthens supplier relationships to keep up with current technology, regardless of whether those suppliers are also competitors.

Price

As part of its strategy, Lenovo continues to use its low-cost labour advantage to slash prices. For instance, to make a leap in market share, it drove relentlessly to undercut every major competitor, including prices, as much as by 30% below its chief competitor, Dell Computer.

Promotion

Lenovo's promotion focused on its product-bundling strategy, consisting of tutorial programs on everything from using the World Wide Web to mastering home finances, and even offering free training to China's first-time users – including home visits. To follow-through with its global branding strategy, the company linked a deal with the International Olympic Committee to be the tech sponsor of the Turin and Beijing Olympic Games.

Distribution

Lenovo developed a powerful distribution network that has become the envy of its competitors with its well-honed supply chain of retail stores across China. That network positions the company comfortably close to customers so that managers maintain a firm handle on the market's current and evolving needs. As part of its global expansion moves, Lenovo also taps IBM for help in selling to large corporations.

Action strategy

Lenovo's remarkable success provides valuable lessons you can use to develop a multifaceted marketing strategy: Part 1 utilizes the marketing mix as a practical structure to develop marketing strategies; Part 2 deals with the external forces that are common to most businesses: customers, competitors, industry, and environment.

Let's begin with the marketing mix.

Part 1 –
Marketing mix

A practical structure to develop marketing strategy

As noted in the Lenovo case, the structure for developing a multi-faceted marketing strategy consists of the product, price, promotion, and distribution, universally referred to as the marketing mix. It serves as one of the most pragmatic and organized techniques for developing competitive marketing strategies.

Figure 3.1, Creating strategies out of the marketing mix, illustrates the framework. Each of the four primary components that comprise the marketing mix signifies a potential driver of your strategy. In turn, under each of the four components you can choose those items that suggest strategy possibilities.

In selecting which components of the marketing mix should spearhead your strategy, do the following:

- Compare your company's performance to that of competitors on each of the selected components and decide if you have a clear-cut competitive advantage.

- Check if the items you picked represent your customers' primary needs or wants, for which they will buy your product rather than a competitive offering.

Product	Price	Promotion	Distribution
Quality	List price	Advertising:	Channels:
Features	Discounts	• Customer and	• Direct
Options	Allowances	trade	salesforce
Style	Payment period	Personal selling:	• Distribution
Brand name	Credit terms	• Incentives	• Dealers
Packaging		• Sales aids	Market coverage:
Sizes		• Samples	• Warehouse
Services		• Training	locations
Warranties		Sales promotion:	• Inventory
Returns		• Demonstrations	control
Versatility		• Contests	systems
Uniqueness		• Premiums	• Physical
Utility		• Coupons	transport
Reliability		• Manuals	
Durability		Telemarketing	
Patent protection		Internet	
Guarantees		Publicity	

Figure 3.1: Creating strategies out of the marketing mix

Applications

In working with the marketing mix, your entire purpose is to single out those areas that would help you build strategies and tactics. In turn, if implemented with skill they could represent a distinctive competitive advantage.

The checklist that follows shows the application of some of the areas of the marketing mix with accompanying actions. (Many of these actions were expertly performed by Lenovo.)

1. Select a feature of your product, such as quality, packaging, options, or features that could represent a competitive advantage and that larger competitors cannot match.

   Action: Employ formal market research or use personal observation to identify possibilities for differentiating your product or service.

2. Commit to quality and service as an organizational priority.

   Action: Initiate programmes that encourage individuals at various functions to strive for quality. These are not one-time motivational talks, but continuous training.

3. Focus on speciality products that command premium prices. Leave the commodity price segment to others, unless you are the low-cost producer.

   Action: Practice segmenting your market for specific product applications. Get closer to your customers and their problems.

4. Establish long-term alliances with customers to grow with them and to build technology and product relationships.

   Action: Encourage trust with customers or suppliers so that sensitive information can be shared for mutual interests. If possible, utilize them to design product features, propose product options, or identify new services.

5. Maintain a market-driven orientation throughout the organization – within all functions – that leads to closer relationships with customers.

   Action: Organize strategy teams made up of functional managers. Then use the teams' strategic marketing plans as lines of communication to respond rapidly to market opportunities. (Strategic marketing planning is discussed in Chapter 5.)

6. Investigate opportunities that complement your long-term objectives.

   Action: Seek joint ventures, licensing, or exporting situations that can expand your presence in existing markets and help extend into new or undeveloped markets.

7. Partner salespeople with customers to provide product solutions to customers' problems.

   Action: Go beyond traditional forms of sales training. Instead, teach salespeople how to think like strategists, so they can help *their* customers achieve a competitive advantage.

8. Identify market niches that are emerging, neglected, or poorly served.

   Action: Reassess how you segment your markets. Search for additional approaches beyond the usual criteria of customer size, frequency of purchase, and geographic location. Look for potential niches related to just-in-time delivery, performance, application, quality, or technical assistance.

Or use any other strategy area from Figure 3.1 that builds a unique competitive advantage for your company.

Part 2 – External forces

Influences common to most businesses

The second part that highlights Lenovo's exceptional performance deals with the external forces that are common to most businesses: customers, competitors, industry, and environment.

Let's see how each contributes to shaping the competitive marketing strategy.

Customers

The customer is the centre of marketing's attention. To produce want-satisfying products and services you must know what your customers want, where they can find what they want, and how to communicate to them that you are able to meet their needs and solve their problems.

Thus, understand your customers – if you expect to sustain growth and maintain a comfortable lead over hard-driving competitors.

Beyond wishing for a brilliant idea to flash into your mind, there is a process you can follow to trigger marketing innovation.

Use the following guidelines for your analysis:

- *Define your customers by demographic, geographic, and psychographic (behavioural) characteristics.* Observe changes in the character of your markets. For instance, look for any unmet customer needs that would enable you to respond rapidly in the form of products, services, methods of delivery, credit terms, or technical assistance. Talk with customers to detect their most troublesome problems and frustrations. Meet with sales people and draw them out on ways to innovate.

- *Examine customer usage patterns or frequency of purchase.* Watch for alternative and substitute products that could represent an opportunity to replace competitive products. Also observe deviations in regional and seasonal purchase patterns. Check for changes from past purchasing and usage practices that could translate into opportunities.

- *Survey selling practices.* Innovations often occur in selling. Stay tuned-in to current trends in promotional allowances, selling tactics, trade discounts, rebates, point-of-purchase opportunities, or seasonal/holiday requirements. Here, again, stay close to sales people for such information. Encourage them to input all behavioural information about perceptions dealing with your product, delivery, company image, complaint handling, and any other factors that influence a sale and contribute to a long-term relationship.

- *Survey channels of distribution.* Examine your distribution methods and look for opportunities to customize services consistent with the characteristics of the segment. Pay attention to warehousing (if applicable) and which areas could be fertile possibilities to innovate, such as with electronic ordering and computerized inventory control systems. Look, too, at the direct marketing channels and the techniques pioneered by such companies as Dell Computer and Gateway. Experiment with other marketing innovations, such as the Internet as a new sales and distribution channel.

- *Look at product possibilities.* Watch for innovative new products and product line extensions to give you an ongoing presence in your existing markets or to gain a foothold in an emerging segment. Seek opportunities to differentiate or add value to products by harnessing new technology in ways that might broaden your customer base and leverage your company's expertise.

- *Explore opportunities to cut costs for you and your customers.* Investigate ways to strengthen quality assurance and introduce new warranties to improve product performance and reliability. Also look for possibilities to replace products or systems, improve internal and external operating procedures, and discover new product applications.

Competitor

Look objectively at competitors and accurately plot their market positions. Armed with factual information, you can then move to a preferred point and concentrate your resources against their weak spots, with the overall aim of creating your own competitive advantage.

Competitor analysis should be viewed from a variety of perspectives:

- **Customer selection**: Single out those competitors with whom your customers conduct business.

- **Competitor segments**: Determine how competitors divide their market.

- **Behavioural purchase patterns**: Learn why customers buy from your competitors and not from you.

- **Competitive strategies**: Find out how competitors develop their strategies against you and how effective they are in attacking or defending a market.

- **Strengths and weaknesses**: Determine competitors' strengths and weaknesses in such areas as product mix, new product development, channels of distribution, promotion, salesforce coverage, and overall managerial capabilities.

In short, understand your competitors by examining customer selection, competitor segmentation, behavioural purchase patterns, and competitor strategies.

Industry

An industry is the sum of many parts, such as: sources of supply, existing competitors, emerging competitors, alternative product and service offerings, and various levels of customers – from intermediate types such as original equipment manufacturers (OEM) to after-market end users.

Within these assorted parts are eleven powerful influences that can affect an industry – and consequently influence how you develop your marketing effort.

1. Current demand for your product

Indicates the demand or usage of your product in sales, units, number of users, share of market, or whatever measurement provides reliable indications of demand and would consequently have an immediate effect on current operations and profitability.

2. Future potential for your product

Uses a timeframe of three to five years to forecast the potential for your product. In turn, that information impacts your decisions to stay in the market, allocate resources to the market, and assess where your product is in its life cycle (introduction, growth, maturity, or decline) before it becomes obsolete and needs replacement.

3. Industry life cycle

Identifies the stage the industry is in in its life cycle. Industries as well as products have cycles, mostly influenced by rapidly changing technologies, emerging markets, and shifts in buyer behaviour.

4. Emerging technology

Specifies which technology is currently available or may be in use even on an experimental basis within the industry, and specifically with competitors. It determines from where the technology is coming and who holds patents or copyrights.

5. Changing customer profiles

Uses segmentation criteria to track any significant changes in demographics, geographics, buyer behaviour, or psychographics (life style) of your existing and future markets.

6. Frequency of new product introductions

Monitors the introduction of new products to determine if there is an industry pattern that can serve as a standard for your own level of product development. Such information helps you judge the ability of your organization to keep pace with the flow of new products.

7. Level of government regulation

Determines if government regulation is increasing or declining; and assesses the impact on your industry and, most important, your company's ability to conform to stringent regulations.

8. Distribution networks

Indicates if there are significant innovations in the use of distribution channels. For instance, is there emphasis on pushing the product through distributors, or pulling the product through the supply chain by influencing the end user, or perhaps eliminating distributors entirely? You can then check if there is evidence of forward integration in which producers are acquiring distributors or vice versa.

9. Entry and exit barriers

Assesses the ease or difficulty of entering and exiting an industry. Entry barriers include the amount of capital investment needed, the extent of economies of scale, access to distribution channels, and opportunities for product differentiation.

Exit barriers cover the length of time needed in the market to honour labour contracts, the length of existing leases, services and parts provided to customers, government regulations, social responsibilities to communities and workers, level of emotional attachment to the business or industry, and outside obligations to warehousing or financial institutions.

10. Marketing innovation

Establishes if there are ground-breaking innovations in use that can result in a competitive advantage for you or your competitors, such as electronic ordering systems, computer-driven diagnostic systems, interactive product demonstrations, new promotional incentives, marketing over the Internet, or creative uses of the salesforce.

11. Cost structures

Evaluates the impact of economies of scale on costs and profits as they relate to new product development, manufacturing, purchasing, R&D, marketing, and distribution. Looks at costs related to applying new technology, flexible manufacturing techniques, the Internet, and warehouse automation. Helps you calculate the potential of your industry and your company's ability to compete at a profit.

Using the above guidelines and developing a workable profile gives you a reliable picture of the overall industry. In turn, such an analysis provides insights into future trends so you can stakeout promising areas for growth.

Environmental

Powerful forces of demographics, economics, natural resources, technology, legislation, and cultural values can make or break marketing efforts for your business. Through environmental analysis, you can judge the impact on strategy in each of the following categories by asking yourself the question, 'What potential does this factor hold for my product or service?'

Demographic

Explosive population growth will occur within poor countries. This issue points to great potential markets for foods, medicines, basic machines, clothing, agricultural products, and various low-technology products.

Economic

With the recovering economies and the continuing intensity of competition from the Pacific Rim and North America, and from a growing number of aggressive East European countries, there will be tremendous pressure to stay competitive. With the continuing trends in innovation, cost reduction, and outsourcing, it will be necessary to determine the impact of all these issues on your local economy – and specifically on the buying behaviour of groups in your geographic segments.

Natural resources

Greater demands for oil and various minerals are slated to pose a serious problem. By the year 2050, several minerals may be exhausted if the current rate of consumption continues. While firms that use these resources face cost increases and potential shortages, for other firms there is the exciting prospect of discovering new sources of materials or alternative forms of energy to replace pressures on existing natural resources.

Technology

The often quoted statistic that 90% of all the scientists who ever lived are alive today sums up the accelerating pace of technological change. Only in the past decade has technology resulted in a tremendous number of new high-tech products, such as the pervasive use of the Internet, and the multitude of audio and video links from workplace to home to other distant locations. New technological advances are changing the way workers are handling their jobs and the way consumers purchase products.

Legislation

Businesses are in various stages of regulation and deregulation and, within the political and legal environment, the number of public interest groups is increasing. These groups lobby government officials and put pressure on managers to pay more attention to minority rights, senior citizen rights, women's rights, and consumer rights in general. They also deal with such areas as cleaning up the environment and protecting natural resources.

Cultural values

Cultural values come and go. The three basic components of culture – things, ideas, and behaviour patterns – undergo additions, deletions, or modifications. Some components die out, new ones are accepted, and existing ones can be changed in some observable way. Thus, any cultural environment today is not exactly the same as it was last year, or what it will be one year hence. The cultural environment, therefore, needs constant monitoring to take advantage of new opportunities.

The following case illustrates many of the concepts and guidelines related to the two parts of a multifaceted marketing strategy: marketing mix and external forces.

NutriSystem

NutriSystem is a foremost organization in the pervasive weight-loss industry. The company has survived many organizational incarnations, encompassing numerous managerial changes, marketing flops, and legal actions. Today it is a thriving leader in its field. Since 2002, when the current management took over a then 30-year-old operation, revenue jumped from $28 million to $413 million and profit from $2.5 million to $55 million. In recognition for its achievements, in 2006 *Forbes Magazine* ranked NutriSystem as No.1 on its list of the Best 200 Small Companies.

The turnaround has not been easy. The company had to find a workable strategy within an industry directed by external fashion and fads, monitored by legislation, and plagued by scams. Then, there were the fickle behaviours of transient customers who stayed for a period of time and would leave for almost any reason, usually triggered by annoyance, boredom, or simply temptation. It's also an industry beleaguered by outlandish promises of dazzling results by companies that do not always fulfill advertised claims, and which in extreme cases become clients for law firms.

NutriSystems' strategies

Using the structure of the marketing mix, NutriSystems emerged with the following strategies:

Product: The company's products consist of small-portion, safe, pre-packaged meals to over-weight individuals. A typical daily regimen includes: oatmeal for breakfast, pasta salad for lunch, a dinner of lasagna with pudding for dessert – all in tiny portions. By taking in fewer calories and replacing simple carbohydrates with whole grains, the average person can lose about two pounds a week. Its products reflect the glycemic index, which ranks carbs by their effect on blood sugar.

With the average stay of about 10 weeks and as part of the product offering, customers can also get weight-loss counseling over the phone.

Outsourcing is also central to NutriSystems' product strategy. All recipe development and food preparation are sent to a group of outside vendors who are responsible for every stage of product development.

Promotion: The company has fine-tuned its promotion efforts to a point that management can set realistic goals for its sales reps. Relying exclusively on direct marketing, its key marketing strategy is to display a series of before-and-after photos of NutriSystem dieters and employ high-profile personalities to present the findings on numerous TV ads and in print media. All ads prominently show a toll-free telephone number shouting for an immediate call-to-action. To back up promotions, NutriSystem controls and closely monitors its own call centre. From 5 a.m. to midnight, 200 telemarketers work the phones. Each sales person is ranked by dollars per call. The top sellers bring in an average $136 per call and typically earn six-figure commissions per year.

Price: Pricing takes a market-driven approach, which is anchored to closely-watched costs and profit goals. Operating out of nondescript buildings for its headquarters and call centre, the company focuses on maximum profitability by maintaining a bare-bones operation and lean staffing. For instance, the overall cost to acquire a customer is around $130, which generates about $700 in revenue, half of which covers NutriSystem's costs for food and shipping.

Distribution: The supply chain is short and direct. There are no grocery stores or other middlemen, and no costly weigh-in centres to eat-up profits. Once customers sign-on for the program, NutriSystem ships them a supply of securely-packaged food through an outside logistics company operating from five warehouses.

Best practices

Keeping in mind the strategy practices illustrated in the Lenovo and NutriSystem cases, now we can arrive at a workable definition of strategy that should serve your business needs:

> *Strategy is the art of coordinating the means (money, human resources, and materials) to achieve the ends (profit, customer satisfaction, and company growth) as defined by company policy and objectives.*

In turn, this primary definition has implications on how you organize your marketing effort and involves virtually every function of your organization. The definition also parallels the way in which you should think of strategic marketing as:

> *A total system of interacting business activities designed to price, promote, and distribute want-satisfying products and services to business-to-business and consumer markets in a competitive environment at a profit.*

So that strategy permeates every part of your organization and involves all company personnel, strategy is further defined and implemented at three levels:

1. **Higher-level corporate strategy**. At this level, direct your company's total resources toward fulfilling company policy without exhausting its resources. Specifically, that means you implement corporate strategy with a view toward the market's long-range growth potential with a minimum expenditure of company resources.

2. **Mid-level strategy**. Here, strategy operates at the division, business unit, department, or product-line level. While contributing to your overall company policy, it is more precise than corporate strategy. It covers a period of three to five years and focuses on achieving quantitative and non-quan-

titative objectives. Specifically, your purpose is to provide for continued growth in four modes:

- Penetrating existing markets with existing products

- Expanding into new markets with existing products

- Developing new products for existing markets

- Launching new products into new markets.

3. **Lower-level strategy or tactics**. This level requires a shorter timeframe than at the two higher levels, usually one-year, and correlates most often with the annual marketing plan. Think of tactics as actions designed to achieve short-term objectives, while complementing your longer-term objectives and strategies. These are precise actions in such areas as: pricing and discounts, advertising media and copy approaches, salesforce deployment and selling aids, distributor selection and training, product packaging and service, and selection of market segments for product launch.

4

How to manage your competitor intelligence

Chapter objectives

Information, intelligence and decision-making

Developing a competitor intelligence system

Competitor intelligence model

Strategy applications

Marketing research techniques

Types of data

Generating primary data

Use agents to improve competitive intelligence results

Best practices

Chapter objectives

After reading this chapter, you should be able to:

1. Apply competitor intelligence techniques to manage your competitive position.

2. Distinguish between the basic methods of primary data collection.

3. Compare the strengths and weaknesses of the principal interview research strategies.

4. Use agents to improve competitive intelligence results.

In the last two chapters, competitor intelligence was singled out as the central ingredient for understanding your market, assessing competitors' intentions and strategies, launching into new markets, and determining how customers respond to your offerings versus those of your competitors. More precisely, it is appropriate to indicate categorically that there is no practical approach to designing a winning strategy without the input of reliable and documented competitive intelligence.

Scores of companies worldwide are discovering that competitor intelligence can be used as a potent strategic weapon. By collecting information in a variety of new ways, organizations find they can better support their basic products, offer new value-added services that distinguish them from their competitors, and create new products and businesses that extend their markets. 'In the next 10 to 15 years, collecting outside information is going to be the next frontier,' stated the late management guru Peter Drucker.

Information, intelligence and decision-making

Today's unyielding marketplace does not allow for a great deal of management by instinct and intuition. Still, many managers feel compelled to utilize that approach because they find management science techniques overwhelming and intimidating.

While it is not easy to work through the quantitative language often accompanying sensitive intelligence, the alternative of 'flying blind' is hardly promising. Thus, a compromise between the two extremes seems to be the answer. That is, instinct and market intelligence can combine for effective business management.

Notwithstanding, in a competitive world the give and take should tilt in favour of scientifically based information to support and streamline your decision-making. To adequately satisfy this need, information sources and flows must be managed. This management can be accomplished by clearly defining your information requirements, which, in turn, will govern how you gather and process information.

The process of building a complex marketing intelligence system may start with this simple thought: 'If I knew exactly what happened in the past and had some insight into what may happen in the future, I would have a better feel for what actions are needed.'

That statement reveals the manager's desire to develop a mechanism to supply meaningful and up-to-date intelligence that can improve decision-making. You should be able to refer questions to a current and consolidated reservoir of information responsive to the 'If I knew...' wishes. Such a reservoir is known as database marketing, and the method and process of inquiry are typical of information systems.

Data mining for effective decision-making

Databases often contain huge masses of data of strategic importance to effective decision-making and strategy development. But how do you access the information? The newest answer is data mining, which is being used both to increase revenues and to reduce costs. Innovative organizations worldwide are using data mining to locate and appeal to higher-value customers, to reconfigure their product offerings, and to increase sales.

Data mining is a computer-based process that uses a variety of analytical tools to discover patterns and relationships in data that may be used to make valid predictions. For example, data mining might determine that males with incomes between $30,000 and $50,000 who subscribe to sports magazines are likely purchasers of a product you want to sell.

Typically, the data to be mined is first extracted from a company's data warehouse into a data mining database. This process generally is not a do-it-yourself project. Numerous companies with the appropriate software are available to install the system in a company.

The following case illustrates the scope of competitor and market intelligence needed to drive business development, product innovation – and overall marketing strategies.

Procter & Gamble

In 2000, P&G launched a totally independent Internet-based company. Known as reflect.com, the business model called for selling cosmetics and hair products customized to the looks and preferences of each woman who shopped on the Internet. Its specific goal was to introduce make-up and shampoos so personalized that no two individuals would get the same items.

Action strategy

Pivotal to making its core strategy come alive, reflect.com managers moved forward with the following actions:

- Acquired finite information about each woman's needs through an interactive question-and-answer process. To execute the strategy, reflect.com allied with an Internet search organization, Ask Jeeves, which specializes in a technology that enables customers to pose questions and receive answers on a website through a natural dialogue.

- Used P&G's research-and-development lab to formulate a truly personalized product and packaging to match each customer's specifications. Each product, in turn, would also contain the buyer's name. Reflect.com managers' envisioned as many as 50,000 unique hair, skin, and make-up combinations from which to tailor unique products. And it would market the product at a cost no greater than high-end merchandise at a department store cosmetic counter.

- Maintained ongoing market analysis to watch over other product offerings, for instance, from new competitors such as web rival, gloss.com, that sells upscale cosmetics with brands that include Calvin Klein and Chanel, to make sure that they will not throw up barriers to impede its progress.

The World Wide Web and the information revolution

The World Wide Web is now the trigger for the explosive level of activity designed to acquire finite information not only of groups but also of individual behaviour. The technology is so pervasive and eye-popping that individuals can surf the Web and do their shopping through secure computer transactions.

Then as customers make inquiries or purchases, hidden files or tags called 'cookies' are deposited on their computers. Software programs then use those files to track and analyze on-line behaviour. Such data becomes the underpinnings to design a product or service offering built around a one-on-one approach.

Britain's ICL illustrates the major innovations of new information technology. For instance, Europeans can order groceries over the Net by scanning product bar codes on computers built into their refrigerators using ICL's technology.

Smart cards allow users to do everything from storing personal information to earning bonus points at retailers. In turn, such information provides vendors with valuable data on usage patterns, expenditures, time of purchase, and numerous other pieces of information that when assembled provide an exacting customer profile.

The information gathering activity is so mammoth that one Web portal, Yahoo!, collects some 400 billion bytes of information every day – the equivalent of a library crammed with 800,000 books – about where visitors click on a site. Armed with the information, it calculates which ads and products appeal most to visitors so it can gain more e-commerce sales.

Developing a competitor intelligence system

Contrary to a common misconception, intelligence systems are not developed with the intention of replacing people with machines. Their purpose is to improve, not replace, decision-making. For example, the intelligence delivered by an information system will guide you in allocating scarce resources in a manner that will optimize profits. For obvious reasons, the cost of intelligence is justifiable only as long as it continues to improve decision-making.

Such an intelligence system can accomplish the following:

- Monitor competitors' actions to develop counter-strategies.
- Identify neglected or emerging market segments.
- Identify optimum marketing mixes.
- Assist in decisions to add a product, drop a product, or modify a product.
- Develop more accurate strategic marketing plans.

Figure 4.1 summarizes what a system can and cannot do for you.

Can do	Cannot do
1. Track progress toward long-term strategic goals	1. Replace managerial judgment
2. Aid in day-to-day decision-making	2. Provide all the information necessary to make an infallible decision
3. Establish a common language between marketing and 'back office' operations	3. Work successfully without management support
4. Consider the impact of multiple environments on a strategy	4. Work successfully without confidence
5. Automate many labour-intensive processes, thus effecting huge cost savings	5. Work successfully without being adequately maintained and responsive to the user community
6. Serve as an early warning device for operations or businesses not on target	
7. Help determine how to allocate resources to achieve marketing goals	
8. Deliver information in a timely and useful manner	
9. Help service customers	
10. Enable you to improve overall performance through better planning and control	

Figure 4.1: Capabilities and limitations of a competitor intelligence system

Competitor intelligence model

The following guidelines show you how to organize the data coming into the system from diverse sources. Whereas an IT manager may be in charge of the technology for maintaining an intelligence system, the responsibility for its usefulness and application sits squarely on the shoulders of the marketing executive – or any manager in charge of devising competitive strategies.

In order to understand the flow of data, you need to examine each of the following sections.

Collecting field data

At the top of the list is the salesforce, which represents one of the most valuable sources of competitor intelligence. When salespeople are trained to observe key events and oriented to believe their input fits into the competitive strategy process, these men and women are first-line reporters of competitor actions.

You can maintain communications with salespeople by periodically travelling with them, by conducting formal debriefing sessions to gain detailed insights behind the competitor actions they observed, and by creating or expanding a section of the salesforce call-reports to record key competitor information.

Collecting published data

There are numerous sources of published information, from small-town newspapers, in which a competitor's presence makes front-page headlines, to large-city or national newspapers and magazines that provide financial and product information about competitors. Monitoring want ads in print and over the Internet provide clues to the types of personnel and skills being sought.

Also, speeches by senior management of competing companies provide valuable insights into other firms' future plans, industry trends, and strategies under consideration. At times it is astonishing how much sensitive information is provided in speeches that are given at a variety of trade shows and professional meetings and that subsequently get into print.

Compiling the data

Additional marketing intelligence can be compiled by interviewing individuals who come in contact with competitors. You can create special forms that capture key events, such as trade shows. Or you can subscribe to clipping services that submit pertinent articles clipped from newspapers and magazines on competitors' activities related to such areas as pricing, new product introductions, distribution, or special promotions.

Cataloguing the data

The varied sources of data come together at this point in the system. Depending on the facilities available to you, the data should be organized and maintained under the overall direction of a senior marketing or sales manager, marketing analyst, manager of marketing intelligence, or marketing research individual.

Digestive analysis

The first four procedures are mechanical ways of collecting, compiling, and cataloguing data. The creative aspects now apply as you begin to synthesize the data to detect opportunities. At this time call in key functional managers from finance, manufacturing, and product development to assist in the analysis.

Communication to strategist

There are various approaches to communicate the synthesized information: including oral reports at weekly staff meetings and the increasingly popular competitor newsletter. The primary purpose of communication is to feed the next section.

Competitor analysis for strategy formulation

The single most important purpose of the entire competitor intelligence system is to develop competitive strategies, which become an integral component of the strategic marketing plan.

Strategy applications

While it is in your best interest to become the driving force behind installing and managing a competitive intelligence system, your next important role is to know where to apply the information to improve performance through enterprising strategies.

For instance, maintaining a strong market presence or expanding into new markets can be viewed through:

1. market segmentation analysis,

2. product life cycle analysis, and

3. new product development.

All of which depend on a solid foundation of reliable market and competitor intelligence.

For *market segmentation analysis,* competitor and marketing intelligence systems can be used to:

- Identify segments as demographic, geographic, and psychographic (lifestyle).

- Determine common buying factors and usage rates within segments.

- Monitor segments by measurable characteristics – for example, customer size, growth rate, and location.

- Assess potential new segments by common sales and distribution channels.

- Evaluate segments to protect your position against inroads by competitors.

- Determine the optimum marketing mix (product, price, promotion, and distribution) for protecting or attacking segments.

For *product life cycle analysis,* system output can be used at the introductory stage to:

- Determine if the product is reaching the intended audience segment and what the initial customer reactions to the offering are.

- Analyze the marketing mix and its various components for possible modifications – for example, product performance, backup service, and additional warranties.

- Monitor for initial product positioning to prospects – that is, to determine if customer perceptions match intended product performance.

- Identify possible points of entry by competitors in such areas as emerging or poorly served segments; and by using product or packaging innovations, aggressive pricing, innovative promotions, distribution incentives, or add-on services.

- Evaluate distribution channels for market coverage, shipping schedules, customer service, effective communications, and technical support.

- Compare initial financial results to budget.

At the *product life cycle* growth stage, system output can be used to:

- Analyze product purchases by market segment.
- Identify the emerging market segments and any new product applications.
- Conduct a competitor analysis and determine counter strategies by type of competitor.
- Adjust the marketing mix to emphasize specific groups; for example, changes in product positioning by shifting from a pull-through advertising strategy directed to end users to a push advertising programme aimed at distributors.
- Decide on use of penetration (low) pricing to protect specific market segments.
- Provide new incentives for the salesforce.
- Monitor financial results against plan.
- Provide feedback on product usage and performance information to R&D, manufacturing, and technical service for use in developing product life cycle extension strategies.

At the *product life cycle* maturity stage, system output can be used to:

- Evaluate differentiation possibilities to avoid facing a commodity type situation, where pricing pressure is prevalent.
- Determine how, when, and where to execute product life cycle extension strategies – for example, finding new applications for the product and locating new market segments.
- Expand product usage among existing market segments or find new users for the product's basic materials.
- Monitor threats to market segments on a competitor-by-competitor basis.
- Evaluate financial performance, in particular profitability. (If all went according to plan you should be in a cash cow stage and generating cash.)

At the *product life cycle* decline stage, output can be used to:

- Evaluate options such as focusing on a specific market niche, extending the market, forming joint ventures with manufacturers or distributors, and locating export opportunities.

- Determine where to prune the product line to obtain the best profitability.

- Monitor financial performance as a means of fine tuning parts of the marketing mix.

- Identify additional spin-off opportunities through product applications, service, or by using new distribution networks that could create an additional product life cycle.

For *new product development,* marketing intelligence system output can be used as a preliminary screening device to:

- Identify potential market segments as an idea generator for new product development.

- Determine the marketability of the product.

- Assess the extent of competitors' presence by specific market segments.

- Develop a product introduction strategy from test market to roll-out.

- Define financial performance.

Marketing research techniques

When you use competitor intelligence to plan your strategies, marketing research provides the primary input to reduce the risks inherent in decision-making. Such research is invaluable during every phase of the marketing process, from the onset of a new product or service idea through the stages of its evolution and market life and, finally, to the decision to discontinue the product or service.

Marketing research, then, is the mechanism to improve the effectiveness of your marketing decisions by furnishing accurate information about consumer needs or problems through which you can base your recommendations.

Market research guidelines

As detailed in the following section, reliable market research comes from two major sources: primary data and secondary data. For you to gain the optimum use for the feedback, market research must be:

1. **Accurate**. At stake are critical decisions affecting expenditures of money, human resources, and time.

2. **Timely**. Events have cycles that, once past, may not occur again or whose opportunities pass to competitors who have seized the moment.

3. **Usable**. Data that cannot be applied is irrelevant. It must fill the gaps of information in your marketing plan.

4. **Understandable**. Information is virtually useless unless you can internalize and interpret it with relative ease and then use the data to develop strategies and tactics.

5. **Meaningful**. If the information lacks importance, if it is not significant but is merely nice-to-know information, the vital contribution of market research to survival and growth is missed.

Finally, marketing research is essential for measuring, evaluating, and projecting various competitive scenarios. A clear understanding of the data plays a key role in maintaining competitive strength in existing markets and in expanding into new growth areas.

Types of data

You can get the data needed for marketing research either by turning to existing information (secondary data) or by generating your own (primary data). Initially, you should avoid a primary research study for reasons of time and cost. Instead, many marketing questions can be answered satisfactorily by utilizing secondary data. Only if this avenue proves to be inadequate should you consider primary research.

The distinction between the two types of data is a matter of purpose and control. Secondary data has been collected for another purpose. That is, you have no control over the gathering, processing, and interpretation. Therefore, check carefully to see how applicable it is to your situation. The unit of investigation may have been different (for example, families instead of households); the sample size may have been insufficient; the wrong people may have been queried; the questions may have been leading; the data may now be obsolete.

Even so, a thorough review of available secondary data is a must before you undertake a primary research project, because this data may provide all the answers you need. For instance, if you must find out who are the heavy users of powdered detergents and where they are located, it would be unwise to collect your own data at great expense. Data of this type is readily available from commercial suppliers. Even if you want to know who are your own ultimate buyers, you don't necessarily need to generate your own information. A professional data-collection organization may already have this information in its files.

Generating primary data

Of course, if you come up with 'what if' questions, secondary data is no longer useful. It cannot address the issues of new product information, reactions to advertising, the impact of alternative pricing approaches, or the effect of a package change, etc.

It then becomes unavoidable to generate your own data for the specific research purpose at hand. To help you do so, you have three major methods at your disposal: experimentation, observation, and interviewing (see table 4.1).

Experimentation

Experimental research looks at the impact of changes for two variables. One is held constant while the other is an experimental variable and is deliberately manipulated to test its effect on the outcome, usually measured in terms of sales. For example, a typical experiment tests different prices which are charged for the same product in different cities to determine the direct effect of price on sales.

To be meaningful, such tests require controlled situations. If influences from extraneous, uncontrollable variables (for example, dealer displays) are found, the data will have to be adjusted accordingly.

Therefore, it is advisable to use control groups, in which no changes are introduced, to ensure the reliability of the experimental research. Each experiment must be designed and tailored to meet the specific needs of your project.

Observation

Should you want to know the reactions of consumers to your product, packaging, advertising, or some other aspect of your marketing mix, observation can supply you with the input. Researcher and marketing manager could personally watch a test to obtain a first-hand look at the consumer's reaction to an intended change before implementing it on a large scale.

Observation involves recording the behaviour of people or the results of such behaviour. At times it can be completed without the knowledge or consent of the subjects, thus allowing them to behave uninhibitedly. Accordingly, learn to interpret meaningful gestures; for example, during prospecting and while observing the purchasing process. There are also sophisticated electronic approaches that use hidden cameras aimed at supermarket aisles to observe non-verbal buying patterns.

However, for everyday use you can conduct a more modest approach by watching body language as part of your overall observation of market and customer behaviour. For example, you could personally observe the behaviour displayed by consumers in selecting toys. In contrast, a surveillance camera or a psychogalvanometer (lie detector) would record consumer reactions.

Auditing and visual assessment, often referred to as 'looking' research, is another kind of observation. By generating a count of the merchandise most recently moved through supermarkets, observation research gives you a capsule overview of the competitive framework for your product at a particular point in time.

As in experimentation – which borrows heavily from observation and interview – observation can be carried out either in the marketplace (traffic counts) or in a laboratory setting (eye movement studies). Whatever the circumstances, you use observation to find out what people do. Its big limitation is, of course, that it cannot tell you why they do what they do.

Interviewing

Interviewing is asking questions of selected respondents who might possess valuable insights and would represent the group under investigation. Such survey research can be conducted formally or informally, structured or unstructured, and disguised. If it is informal, the results cannot be extended to the underlying population.

If it is structured, a formal list of questions (questionnaire) is used. If it is disguised, the true purpose of the research is concealed from the interviewee. An example of an informal, unstructured, undisguised questioning technique is the focus group interview (see page 84), while a mail questionnaire is a formal, structured, disguised technique.

These various characteristics explain why interviewing is by far the most widely and most frequently used approach in primary data generation. It is not as cumbersome and expensive as experimentation, and it digs beneath the observed behavioural surface in perception and motivation.

To get at the truth, however, a great deal of skill is required in executing a survey, because it is subject to even more human bias than either experimentation or observation. Bias on the part of both the interviewer and the respondent add to any inherent defects in the wording or sequence of questions.

Interview research can be extended over a period of time to monitor changes in your competitive environment. Or it can provide a one-time snapshot of your market highlighting, for instance, the impact of a particular advertising campaign. Like the other two methods, you can interview either in the field (in supermarkets, shopping centres, or homes) or in the laboratory (inviting selected consumers into a research facility).

A key rule in interviewing is to ask only necessary questions, because every additional question takes time, increasing the risk of consumer refusal. You should, therefore, refrain from asking questions that interest you personally but contribute little to the understanding of the subject at hand.

Why	How	Where	Data collection techniques	Examples	Check points
Experimental research					
To understand the association between two variables that may suggest a causal relationship	Manipulate the independent variable Measure the dependent variable Control certain extraneous variables and randomize as many others as possible	In a laboratory situation	Personal interviews Telephone interviews Mail surveys Group discussions Depth interviews	Assess the effect of a promotional campaign Test the effect of product trial on future purchase behaviour Determine the effectiveness of a TV commercial Select the most appropriate subscription plan for a magazine Study the effect of a consumer education programme on product sales	Needs careful pre-planning Rigorous problem definition Precise identification and definition of variables Use of control groups Adjustment for errors due to extraneous variables
Observation research					
To observe and record consumer behavioural responses to marketing stimuli	Set up situation for consumer to take action Station observers or observational mechanisms to record consumer reactions Evaluate results	In the marketplace Under simulated field conditions in a laboratory-type situation	Watching and recording by trained interviewers or technicians Electronic equipment, videotape recorders, audiometers, and lie detectors	Conduct periodic store audits to track brand shares of a product Observe customer shipping patterns in a supermarket Record pupil movements in a print copy test Evaluate prototype toys by observing children at play with them	Needs careful pre-planning Rigorous problem definition Simulation of test conditions as close as possible to actual market conditions Checking of customers to make sure they understand the tasks you want them to perform

Why	How	Where	Data collection techniques	Examples	Check points
Interview research					
To measure and understand consumer behaviour, attitudes, or images related to a given marketing problem	Collect data from target consumers Compile data Analyze data Interpret results Conclude and recommend action plan	In marketplace with relevant consumers In the laboratory	Personal interviews Telephone interviews Mail surveys Group discussions Depth interviews	Collect demographic data on current customers Determine usage rates of company products Determine image of corporation among product non-users Discuss merits and shortcomings of products available in a given market education programme on product sales	Needs careful pre-planning Rigorous problem definition Checking to make sure correct consumer group is surveyed Limitation of interviews to brief period Elimination of bias in key questions

Table 4.1. Highlights of the three basic methods of primary data collection

Three approaches

Depending on the nature of your research task, the amount of money and time available, and the accessibility of the target group to be surveyed, conclusive interview research may take one of three forms:

1. **In-person interview**: Interviewer questions respondent face-to-face:

   a) in the privacy of the interviewee's home or office, or

   b) in a central location by intercepting the consumer in a shopping mall or on the street.

2. **Telephone interview**: The interviewer conducts a survey over the telephone:

   a) in a local market, or

   b) over nationwide telephone lines.

3. **Mail interview**: Survey questionnaire is mailed to selected respondents and returned by mail.

	In-person	Telephone	Mail
Flexibility in data collection	Most flexible; can use visual aids, depth probes, various rating scales; can even alter direction of interview while still in progress	Fairly flexible, although visual aids and extensive rating scales cannot be used	Least flexible, but pictures and rating scales that do not require investigator assistance may be incorporated into a questionnaire; too many open-minded questions reduce response rate
Quality of data obtainable	Fairly extensive data may be obtained, subject to respondent-investigator rapport	Generally limited by short duration of interview	Long questionnaires adversely affect response rate and are not recommended
Speed of data collection	Process of personally contacting respondents is time-consuming	Data available almost instantaneously; ideal for ad-recall and similar studies	Delays result from slow and scattered returns
Expense of data collection	Generally most expensive	Less expensive than in-person interview	Least expensive, depending on return rate
Investigator bias	Respondent-investigator interaction may significantly modify responses	Investigator bias, while present, is less serious than with in-person interview	No investigator bias
Lead time for respondents	Need to respond quickly to questions may result in incomplete or inaccurate data	Same problem as with in-person interviews	Respondents have time to think things over and do calculations to provide more detailed and accurate information
Sampling considerations	In-person interviews require detailed addresses of all respondents; problem may sometimes be overcome by using area and systematic sampling procedures	Problems resulting from imperfections in telephone directory may be controlled to some extent by using 'random digit dialling' or other computerized procedures	Mailing list is required; samples generated from unreliable lists introduce substantial selection bias
Non-response bias	Refusal rate is generally somewhat higher than with telephone interview	Callbacks can reduce non-response bias and are fairly inexpensive	Non-response bias could be very serious in cases where those who return the questionnaire differ substantially from those who do not

	In-person	Telephone	Mail
Sequence bias	No serious problem; investigator can record any changes respondents wish to make to answers to previous questions as interview progresses	Same as with in-person interviews	Respondents can see entire questionnaire and modify their responses to individual questions
Anonymity of responses	In-person, eye-to-eye contact may stifle frank interchange on sensitive issues	Obtaining frank responses is a problem, although less so than in in-person interview situations	Frank responses on sensitive issues can be obtained by guaranteeing anonymity
Identity of respondents	Easily available for future reference	Name and telephone number are available for future reference	May not be available in many cases; questionnaire may even have been filled out by someone other than intended respondent
Field control	Difficult and expensive	Centralized control is no problem; better-quality data result	Generally not a problem
Difficulty of reaching certain segments of population	The very rich are hard to reach, and investigators dodge very poor areas; most working men and women cannot be reached during normal working hours	Non-telephone-owning households cannot be reached; most working men and women are unavailable unless interviews are conducted in the evening and at weekends	Individuals with a low literacy level cannot be reached
Geographic coverage	Generally limited by cost considerations	Centralized telephone facilities permit wide coverage at reasonable cost	Geographic coverage is no problem
Investigator assistance	Easily available to explain instructions, provide help with unfamiliar terms and research procedures	Available, although not to the same extent as in in-person interviews	Not available; instructions may be misinterpreted; incomplete answers or blanks are fairly common

Table 4.2: Comparison of relative strengths and weaknesses of the three principal interviewing techniques

In choosing one approach over another, look not only at your budget and timeframe, but also at your likely rate of response and your response bias. The rate of response is the ratio of those who respond to the total number of people contacted. It is subject to a possible non-response bias because people who are not responding may differ substantially from those who do. If this discrepancy is significant, a question may arise as to whether the results are representative.

Response bias, on the other hand, is any distortion in the answers given due to misinterpretation of the questions – or by deliberate misrepresentation. You will want to keep the rate of return as high, and the response bias as low as the constraints of time and budget will allow.

Table 4.2 represents a comparison of the three interviewing techniques on the basis of a variety of criteria. It is designed to assist you in examining their relative merits and choosing the approach best suited to your particular research objectives.

In-person interviewing: Flexibility with depth

In-person interviewing produces not only a relatively high rate of response, but also an unusually high proportion of usable responses. It is the most flexible of the techniques, in that it can respond spontaneously to the unique conditions of each interview and also incorporate a variety of visual cues such as facial expressions, gestures, and body language.

Further, it allows for follow-up questions to clarify and to specify additional answers. Once a respondent agrees to interview in this mode, a considerable amount of time can be spent and extensive information obtained.

On the other hand, in-person interviews are the most expensive questioning technique and can be rather time-consuming to complete because they involve travel. Unless the interviews are conducted in the evening or during weekends, most respondents would most likely be unemployed or retired persons. Geographic coverage is obviously limited by travel time and expense.

Careful training and instructions can moderate the influence that the interviewer might exert over the interviewee (intentionally or inadvertently). To prevent investigators from cheating or falsifying reports, supervisors would verify a certain percentage of questionnaires by contacting respondents.

All things considered, in-person interviewing is, in most instances, the best research method because it combines flexibility with depth and visual monitoring.

Telephone interviewing

If the nature of your study does not require consumer exposure to exhibits or product samples, you could interview by phone. In contrast to in-person interviewing, in which control and supervision of the data-gathering process are difficult and expensive, calling interviewees from a central location provides a great deal of control.

Phone interviewing is the least time-consuming of the three questioning techniques. It is generally less costly than face-to-face interviewing, even though it remains more expensive than mail (depending on the response rate). Interviewers can conduct the survey while sitting at a computer terminal, read the questions from the screen, and type in the responses directly. This direct input eliminates the time-consuming task of coding and keypunching questionnaire data.

Using the telephone, you can survey a relatively large number of people within a short period of time. This makes the telephone query particularly suitable for measuring customer reaction to your product and that of a competitor.

With telephone interviewing, the response rate is good and callbacks are easy. Also, travel is eliminated and interviewer bias is reduced. However, you cannot ask intricate or intimate questions over the phone without the risk of people hanging up on you.

There is obviously a limit to the amount of information you can obtain in this way, since the maximum amount of time a person is willing to spend on the phone with an interviewer has been found to be 30 minutes. It may actually be considerably shorter, depending on the subject matter. Respondents may give incomplete or inaccurate information in an effort to get the interview over with.

Nevertheless, because of ease of administration, speed of response, flexibility, and wide coverage, phone interviews are rapidly gaining in popularity among marketers.

Mail surveys: Large scale, low cost

Although it is the slowest technique in the fieldwork stage, and the most susceptible to internal questionnaire bias, mail survey research offers the most cost-effective method available, potentially generating input from many people at relatively little cost. No interviewing staff are required, and no training or travel expenses are incurred to reach people in relatively inaccessible places.

The respondent can answer the questionnaire at his or her convenience and has time to look up any necessary information. There is no interviewer bias, and questions of a personal, embarrassing, or ego-involving nature (for example, on the use of hair dyes, contraceptives, or feminine hygiene products) are answered more readily through anonymous mail questionnaires.

Probably the most serious problem with mail surveys is motivating people to fill out the questionnaires. If the response rate is less than 20%, it will raise questions about how truly representative your results are with respect to the underlying population. To increase your response rate, you should follow-up your original sample by sending them another copy of your questionnaire with a different cover letter. This action tends to increase returns significantly.

Another drawback to mail interviewing is that you never know for sure whether the questionnaire is actually filled out by the intended respondent. This task may be assigned to another family member or a secretary who might misunderstand or misinterpret some questions.

In spite of these handicaps, mail surveys are widely used because they can reach thousands of participants at a reasonable cost, offer wide geographic coverage, and can address issues that would otherwise be too sensitive.

Focus group interviews

Focus group interviews are a flexible, versatile, and powerful tool for the decision-maker. These interviews can furnish you with valuable information on a variety of competitive and marketing problems in a short span of time and at a nominal cost.

However, you should keep in mind their limitations. Focus groups are a qualitative research, not a quantitative technique and should not be a device for headcounting. The results of focus group interviews cannot be projected to your target market at large. They may not even be representative and, certainly, cannot replace the quantitative research that will supply you with the necessary numbers.

But the interviews can improve the quality of your quantitative research significantly.

When there is no time for a well-planned formal project, you can call upon this technique to supply factual and perceptual input for making reasoned decisions, which otherwise would have to rely exclusively on executive suite conjecture.

Focus group interviewing involves the simultaneous interviewing of a group of individuals – physicians, homemakers, executives, purchasing agents, or any other group of potential buyers or specifiers representative of your market. A session is usually conducted as a casual round-table discussion with six to ten participants.

Fewer than six individuals pose the danger of participants feeling inhibited. More than ten could result in some members not being heard. The idea, of course, is to get input from everybody. Although the length of a focus group interview varies, an average session lasts about two hours.

Travelling around a region or the country in a week, you can collect a good demographic and geographic cross-section of opinions. Thus, focus groups offer a quick and relatively inexpensive research technique.

Use focus group interviews to:

- Diagnose your competitor's strengths and weaknesses.
- Spot the source of marketing problems.
- Spark new product lines.
- Develop questionnaires for quantitative research.
- Find new uses for your products.
- Identify new advertising or packaging themes.
- Test alternative marketing approaches.
- Streamline your product's positioning.

The key figure in a focus group interview is the moderator who introduces the subject and keeps the discussion on the predetermined topic. The moderator could be you or someone employed by an outside marketing research firm. The job of moderator is not an easy one and much preparation is necessary, but the information obtained can be substantial and well worth the effort.

Use agents to improve competitive intelligence results

Agents are your eyes and ears at conferences, trade shows, and even at your competitors' locations. They go beyond the raw numbers, charts, surveys, benchmarking, and the other intelligence gathering techniques.

They explore the human side of competitive intelligence by reporting on the behaviours and personalities of key individuals. Their primary tool to dig for information is personal interaction and observation. Agents also screen and interpret events, news, and validate or dismiss information gathered by other means. Before moving forward and employing agents, however, observe a few general cautions:

- Make certain that you are not violating ethical and legal guidelines. And check if you are adhering to your company's policies.

- Assess prospective agents' motivations, personality traits, and talents. Then, you can determine in what capacity to employ them. For instance, some individuals' only interest is in money, with minor interest in obtaining accurate information about the competitor's true situation. In such cases, question their integrity and use great care in using them.

- Develop a clear idea about the information you seek. Then make certain they are clear about what you want.

The following represents categories of agents, along with suggestions on how to use them.

Native agents

Native agents are the types of individuals with whom you would normally interact during professional gatherings. They tend to voluntarily share company information to satisfy their personal interests, such as making new industry contacts and advancing their careers.

Often, they are somewhat uncaring about the security of their companies; or their own management simply does not caution them about the dangers of revealing company secrets.

You will find native agents in a variety of places:

- Trade shows serve as fertile venues for gathering intelligence from those individuals. It is also a place where competitors typically reveal extensive information through elaborate demonstrations about their products and freely distribute literature overflowing with facts about pricing, back-up services, logistics, product specifications, and so on.

- Also, key individuals from competitors' organizations often present technical papers at open meetings, which detail sensitive information about upcoming products, services, and even market-entry plans. Then there is the Q&A period that usually follows where the speaker, trying further to impress an audience, pours out more information.

- Another prime area for intelligence gathering is the familiar hospitality suite at trade shows and professional meetings where alcohol and talk flow freely. It's a spot where security is often lax and everyone's guard is down.

Inside agents

Inside agents work for competitors. In many cases, they may have been bypassed for promotion, feel under-paid and under-appreciated, relegated to an insignificant job, or generally pushed aside in a variety of political or power struggles within the organization.

They feel abused and see their careers languishing unless they make some bold move. They may also find themselves surrendering to financial pressures to keep family and self whole. And their attitude may be now-or-never.

You need to assess such individuals carefully for their stability and determine how to use them judiciously. Obviously, you want their information, within the bounds of ethical and legal guidelines.

Beyond personal observations, you would employ inside agents for their expertise to sort out meaningful information from scientific and professional journals, industry studies, or from innovative projects described in articles and professional papers written by the competitors' employees.

Product literature and product specification sheets readily available at trade shows and meetings are packed with tremendous detail. Your agents should be able to interpret the data for meaningful intelligence.

In-house company newsletters and news releases contain a fountain of information about individuals who left a competitor's employment and may have moved to the consulting circuit. If approached, these former employees may be willing to reveal information – unless specific contractual restrictions apply.

Press releases may include new employee announcements along with job descriptions, contracts and awards received, training programs available, office or factory openings or closures, as well as specific news that reveal competitor's activities. Here, again, your inside agent could handily provide useful interpretations.

Beyond the above listing, there is the continuing flow of rumours from customers and suppliers that your agent can sort out and verify. Additionally, there are local sources worth tapping, such as banks, local trucking companies, and real estate offices.

Double agents

These agents try to extract intelligence about your company. Stay alert to their intentions. Once identified, you could attempt to turn them around and get them working on your behalf.

They would then serve in the same capacity as inside agents. Here, too, you can assume double agents seek lavish rewards and may even show similar personality traits and motivations as inside agents. However, it is in your best interest to exercise caution. That is, determine the veracity of these individuals, the reliability of their information, and how long you can expect them to remain loyal to your cause. Once again, make certain of not violating ethical, legal, or policy guidelines.

Expendable agents

These agents are your own people who are deliberately fed inaccurate information, which is disseminated in a variety of ways to cause competitors to make wrong decisions. These contrived leaks take many forms.

For example: Passing fabricated information about new product features through sales reps who come in contact with competitors' reps; product managers who pass out false dates about a product launch that would disrupt a competitor's plans.

In spite of your possible discomfort when undertaking such activities, look at the situation from strictly a strategist's viewpoint. Misinformation needs distribution to divert competitors from opposing your indirect strategy moves.

You thereby preserve your company's hard-won market position, control the needless expenditure of financial and human resources fighting unnecessary market battles, and avoid compromising your strategies.

Living agents

These agents usually return with credible information. They are generally experienced, talented, and loyal individuals who can gain access to, and become intimate with, a competitor's high-level executives. They sit in a position to learn their plans and observe movements. These individuals are truly the eyes and ears and often enjoy the closest and most confidential relationships.

Perhaps the one unsettling issue to cope with when using agents – but certainly worth knowing – is which of your employees knowingly or inadvertently passes on your company's information directly or indirectly to competitors. Eventually, those individuals are exposed and you can obtain valuable clues about what motivated them to those acts.

Another concern: Engaging in such stealth activities is usually contrary to the type of practices most managers care to undertake. Again, think of business intelligence as essential to running a company in a highly competitive environment. Above all, it is indispensable to the development and integrity of competitive strategies.

Best practices

To fully benefit from competitor intelligence (CI), follow these guidelines set out below:

1. CI must be *accurate*: critical decisions affecting expenditures of money, human resources, and time are at stake.

2. CI must be *timely*: events have time cycles. Past a certain point an opportunity may not occur again – or competitors may seize the opportunity.

3. CI must be *usable*: data without application becomes irrelevant.

4. CI must be *understandable*: information that cannot be interpreted with relative ease by the average manager and then applied to developing strategies and tactics is nearly useless.

5. CI should be *meaningful*: if it cannot be translated into scenarios of strategies, it's just nice-to-know information.

5

How to manage your strategic marketing plans

Chapter objectives

The strategic marketing plan: a document for success

Marketing plan: one year

Best practices

Chapter objectives

After reading this chapter, you should be able to:

- Identify the steps in the strategic marketing planning process.

- Develop a long-term strategic direction – or mission statement.

- Identify objectives and strategies with long-term implications.

- Develop a portfolio of products and markets based on the strategic direction.

- Identify planning techniques to develop business-building tactics.

There is growing evidence that the world economies are on the verge of a powerful new surge of innovation. Leading this trend is the world-shaking information revolution and what is now known as the Internet economy, which permeates virtually every sector of most world economies. The drivers of change are the following:

- The information revolution continues to boost productivity across most industries. Over the next decade, information-reliant companies in finance, media, and wholesale and retail trade will change the most.

- A surge of major technology breakthroughs will create entirely new industries over the next ten years.

- Increasing globalization will provide simultaneously much larger markets and tougher foreign competitors. The result: companies will have even more incentive to innovate while cutting costs.

- Countries that follow policies that encourage innovation, free trade, and open financial systems will enjoy a competitive edge.

- Businesses that master the new technologies will be able to count on better profits and bigger market share.

One system that binds all those drivers of change is a workable planning system. To support that proposition, consider the following penetrating evidence:

Two-thirds of rapid-growth firms have written business plans, according to PricewaterhouseCoopers Trendsetter survey. The survey also reveals that over the past two years, firms with written plans grew faster, achieved a higher proportion of revenues from new products and services, and enabled chief executives to manage more critical business functions than those firms whose plans were unwritten. Additionally, growth firms with a written business plan have increased their revenues 69% faster over the past five years than those without a written plan.

As further documentation that planning remains the indispensable duty and responsibility of managers at all levels of authority, consider the stirring headlines from a *Business Week* cover story:

'Strategic Planning – It's Back!

Re-engineering? Cost-cutting? Been there, done that.

Now, strategy is king for real growth.'

The story cites four key issues related to planning and strategy:

1. Strategy is again a major focus for higher revenues and profits – and to hatch new products, expand existing business, and create new markets.

2. Business strategy is the single most important management issue and will remain so into the next decade.

3. Democratizing the strategy process is only achieved by handing it over to teams of line and staff managers from different disciplines.

4. Creating networks of relationships with customers, suppliers, and rivals is the strategy of choice to gain greater competitive advantage.

With those convincing validations, acquiring expertise in developing and managing a strategic marketing plan is essential for any manager, regardless of job function, who contributes in any way to hatching new products, expanding existing business, and creating new markets. Assuming such responsibilities come close to describing your current situation, the central aim here is to help you grasp the concepts and apply the techniques of modern strategic marketing planning in a competitive environment.

Bottom line: Properly executed, strategic market planning can shape a vision of what the future of your organization would look like. It searches the past and measures performance. It examines the culture of an organization and probes the strengths and weaknesses of people, equipment, and systems.

In its broadest dimension strategic marketing planning sets in motion actions that can impact the economy in which you operate and the long-term prosperity of your organization. In its personal dimension, a well-developed plan can positively affect your career prospects.

Therefore, attempting to make any sense out of such trends requires an organized plan that pulls together the vast in-flow of market information. In turn, the plan provides a focal point at which all business activities converge into a convenient housing where opportunities are organized with vision, creativity, and innovation.

Ultimately, a planning system will transform three major elements of any business:

- Relationships to customers and business partners
- Informational flow and its impact on relationships among workers within a company
- Internal processes and operations.

The following case illustrates how one company used strategic marketing planning to identify long-term opportunities and manage day-to-day operations.

Emerson Electric

This company makes a host of electrical, electromechanical, and electronic products, many of which are used to control gases, liquids, and electricity. What distinguishes this well-run company from the herd is its dazzling record of 38 uninterrupted years of increased earnings. During those highly competitive growth years, Emerson staunchly endured the challenges of low-cost Brazilian, Korean, and Japanese competitors.

Several factors contributed to Emerson's success:

1. Management recognized, early on, that low-cost, aggressive competitors would remain a permanent part of the global scene and would intensify into the next decade.

2. Management exerted the discipline to secure cost-efficient operations at every level of the organization.

3. Management demonstrated its flexibility to focus on growth markets and exit those segments with little chance of turning a profit, such as defence and construction, and niche businesses such as gardening tools.

4. It realized that cost cutting was only one part of the success equation to sustain growth; the other, that strategic marketing planning should function as the operating system for managing both long-term objectives and day-to-day operations.

A single example sums up Emerson's accomplishments: A decade ago a Japanese plant could offer temperature sensors for washing machines for 20% below Emerson's prices. Today, Emerson's costs are below the Japanese, and the company has regained market share. Rigorous planning, then, is at the heart of Emerson's system for managing growth.

Action strategy

What can you learn from the Emerson case?

Like Emerson, you can utilize strategic marketing planning to grow present markets, spot growth markets, recognize new product innovations, and stay alert to new opportunities.

The following checklist (details are presented later in this chapter) will help you zero in on viable prospects for growth. Once identified and prioritized, you can convert them into long and short-term marketing objectives, strategies, and tactics.

1. **Present markets**. To identify the best opportunities for expanding present markets, you should:

   - Look for approaches to increase product usage by your current customers and redefine market segments where there are changes in customers' buying patterns. Work jointly with customers on innovative ideas to reformulate or repackage the product according to their specific needs. Identify new uses (applications) for your product. Reposition the product to create a more favourable perception over rival products and investigate where to expand into new or unserved market niches. Also, determine how to displace competition – a particularly significant move in no-growth markets.

2. **Customers**. To identify the best opportunities for expanding your customer base, you should:

   - Improve or expand distribution channels. Refine your pricing strategies to coordinate with market-share objectives. Enrich your communications, including advertising, sales promotion, Internet, and publicity, and deploy the salesforce to target new customers with high potential.

Enhance customer service, including technical service and complaint handling and identify changes in trade buying practices, where the buying power may have shifted from manufacturer to distributor or to end-user.

3. **Growth markets**. To identify the major growth markets, you should:

   - Target key geographic locations, specifying which markets or user groups represent the greatest long-term potential. Investigate emerging businesses and acquire new users for your product.

4. **New product development**. To give priority to the best candidates for new product and service development that will impact on immediate and long-range opportunities, you should:

   - Focus on new products that can be differentiated and that have the potential for an extended life cycle. Search for ways to diversify into new or related products, product lines, and/or new items or features. Examine techniques to modify products by customer groups, distribution outlets, or individual customer applications. Work on improving packaging to conform to customers' specifications and to distinguish your product from its rivals and also establish new value-added services.

5. **Targets of opportunity**. To focus on areas outside your current market segment or product line, not included in the other categories, you should:

   - Be innovative and entrepreneurial in your thinking. However, to be somewhat practical, determine how far your company can realistically diversify from its core business and still retain its vitality.

If you were to consider the strategic planning process used by Emerson Electric as a flow chart, it would appear as in Figure 5.1.

The strategic marketing plan: a document for success

Figure 5.1: The strategic marketing plan

The top row of four boxes shown in Figure 5.1 represents the strategic plan section of the strategic marketing plan. The strategic plan is defined as the managerial process of developing and maintaining a strategic fit between the organization and changing market opportunities. It relies on developing:

1. a strategic direction or mission statement,

2. objectives and goals,

3. a growth strategy, and

4. business portfolio plans.

The bottom row of boxes represent the one-year marketing plan. It begins with:

5. a situation analysis of a specific product or market,

6. an evaluation of opportunities,

7. a list of short-term objectives,

8. a set of strategies and tactics to achieve the objectives, and

9. the financial controls and budgets to monitor performance.

To fully understand how to prepare a successful strategic marketing plan, let's examine each section in detail.

Strategic direction

Think of your strategic direction as the mission or vision statement of the company, product line, or individual product. It is the long-range philosophy of a business unit. It reflects a strategic vision of what your product or business can become as you look forward in time for three to five years. As you think about your strategic direction, consider the following:

- What are your distinctive areas of expertise?

- What business should you be in over the next three to five years?

- What types or categories of customers will you serve?

- What customer functions are you likely to satisfy as you see the market evolve?

- What technologies will you use to satisfy customer/market needs?

- What changes are taking place in markets, consumer behaviour, competition, environment, culture, and the economy?

The point of this exercise is that the responsibility for defining a strategic direction no longer belongs only to upper management. Managers from various departments – marketing, product development, manufacturing, finance, and sales – contribute to the overall strategic direction of a business by asking, 'What business should I be in for my individual product?'

Therefore, develop a strategic direction by looking out the window toward inevitable change, not into a mirror that reflects existing patterns. The effort assumes that your organization exhibits a distinguishing characteristic of a market-driven, rather than a product-driven orientation. Table 5.1 gives examples of how these opposite characteristics differ in their organizational orientation.

Product-driven orientation	Market-driven orientation
Railroad company	Transportation company
Oil company	Energy company
Baby food manufacturer	Child care business
Cosmetics company	Beauty, fashion, health company
Computer manufacturing company	Information processing company
Electrical wire manufacturer	Energy transfer business
Vacuum cleaner manufacturer	Cleaner environment business
Valve company	Fluid control company

Table 5.1: Shaping a strategic direction: product-driven versus a market-driven orientation

The following example illustrates how a strategic direction or mission would be written.

Dow Chemical

Dow Chemical's strategic direction for one of its agricultural herbicide products formally read, 'Chemical control of brush on rights-of-way.' This product-driven orientation was too shortsighted and came across more as a product definition than a strategic vision.

When revised to reflect a broader market-driven focus that would drive future product and market development, it read:

> 'Provide high quality products and services to meet vegetation management goals on rights-of-way, industrial, municipality, and aquatic/wetland sites at a profit. Products and services may include chemical, mechanical, application, distribution, consultation, and establishment of desirable vegetation.'

Notice how expansive the statement is and how it defines potential markets and product/market development. In other words, it creates a vision.

Guided by such a statement, managers could expand their vision and direct the product line into innovative product systems, technologies, and ultimately expand their hold on existing markets and launch into new markets.

99

Refining your vision

The above example of strategic direction is no mere play on words. Rather, it has a practical application in helping to shape objectives, strategies, and a portfolio of products and markets.

How far should your thinking go toward a market-driven orientation (Table 5.1)?

It is best to initially think as far toward that orientation as possible, and then come back to a more comfortable position somewhere between the two extremes of a product-driven and market-driven orientation. That position is usually based on the following factors:

1. The culture of the organization, which is exhibited within a broad range of behaviours from conservative to aggressive.

2. The availability of human, material, and financial resources for maintaining existing business functions and for investing in future growth.

3. The amount of risk that management is willing to assume in going into debt.

4. The degree of environmental change that is likely to influence market behaviour.

5. The threat of competitive activities and their impact on survival and growth.

If you have managerial responsibility for your company, business unit, or product line, then responsibility for conceptualizing a mission or strategic direction begins with you. As such, you are no longer a victim of a narrow focus that ends up with mature products, price wars, and other competitive conflicts. The broader market-driven viewpoint permits you to think more expansively about markets and customer needs – not just individual products.

Objectives and goals

When developing objectives and goals, your primary guideline is that they have a strategic focus. That is, objectives should broadly impact your business and correlate with your strategic direction.

Further, your objectives should contain quantitative and non-quantitative statements and cover a timeframe of three to five years.

This time period is reasonable for most businesses: short enough to be realistic and achievable in an increasingly volatile marketplace; yet long enough to be visionary about the impact of new technologies,

g

changing behavioural patterns, the global marketplace, emerging competitors, and changing demographics.

The following example of a joint U.S. and German car parts manufacturer illustrates specific ways in which quantitative and non-quantitative objectives and goals are stated.

Quantitative objectives and goals

- Attain net sales of $37.0 million by the year 200x within the following categories:

Categories	Net Sales ($ mil)	Mix (%)
Distributor	13.0	35.1
Corporate brand (direct)	6.5	17.6
Generic	7.0	18.9
National accounts	5.5	14.8
Military	3.0	8.1
Export sales	2.0	5.5
Total	**37.0**	**100.0**

- Launch 200 new products on a quarterly basis over the next three years, including electrical, front end, brake, air conditioning, and power train.

- Maintain 60 or more dedicated distributors strategically located worldwide to achieve sales objectives.

- Improve customer satisfaction to 94.5%, as measured by the Customer Service Index base period of 2000-01.

- Utilize as a marketing mix element an effective supply and distribution system for the potential launch of existing products into new market segments.

- Develop a prototype of an Internet-based ordering and diagnostic information system for use with distributors by the fourth quarter of 2008.

While some managers resist the use of non-quantitative objectives, there are occasions where long-term market and internal obstacles need to be overcome. In those cases numbers cannot always be attached to objectives. Therefore, it is appropriate to use dates and reporting periods to show progress. In combination, the use of quantitative and non-quantitative objectives allows for the most accurate and effective planning.

Growth strategies

Objectives and goals indicate what you want to accomplish. Growth strategies deal with how, or what actions you are going to take, to achieve those objectives. The major guideline is this:

For each objective there must be a corresponding strategy. If you cannot come up with a strategy for a particular objective, perhaps the so-called objective is not one at all. Rather, it may be a strategy for some other objective.

Strategies are divided into two categories: internal and external. For example:

Internal strategies

These strategies relate to marketing, manufacturing, R&D, distribution, and pricing, as well as to existing and new products, market research, packaging, customer services, credit, finance, sales activities, and organizational changes.

External strategies

These refer to such possibilities as joint ventures, licensing agreements, new distribution networks, emerging market segments, and any opportunities for diversification – if diversification fits the company's strategic direction.

Car parts manufacturer

Internal strategies

- Install an online ordering program that links the top 80 distributors' inventories with independent repair shops.

- Complete the upgrade of the Manchester depot and launch just-in-time delivery service to distribute within 125 miles of the facility.

- Execute a new warranty administration program that is equitable to the company, distributors, and end-user customers, with a timing of 15 days for claims disposition, compared with the current 21 days.

- Implement a quality improvement initiative consisting of continuing education programmes. Also establish indices of performance levels in accordance with new corporate objectives.

External strategies

- Establish quality teams to review causes of errors and recommend corrective action.

- Form joint venture with (name of company) to increase total market share in selected fuel and cooling systems components, resulting in regional sales of $10.4 million and 22% market share.

- Establish an image for high-performance parts in the after-market by establishing 125 new performance centre dealers in key segments of North America, United Kingdom, and Germany.

- Establish teleconferencing sessions with field sales to monitor competitive activities and activate a quick response.

It is also appropriate here to distinguish between a strategy and a tactic. A strategy is a longer-term action to achieve a long-term objective. A strategy usually affects the functional areas of the organization, such as manufacturing, product development, and finance. It concerns the broader aspects of new markets and distribution systems.

On the other hand, a tactic is a shorter-term action to achieve a short-term objective. It is a subset of a strategy and is usually concerned with local issues of more limited impact, such as a single product being launched in a target market segment with specific promotional activities. In practice, a single long-term objective could be accomplished through four or five strategies with six to ten related tactics.

Business portfolio

A business portfolio (fourth box of Figure 5.1) contains a listing of all existing markets and products, and all potential new markets and products that are feasible within the next three to five years and match your company's strategic direction. Generally, the broader the scope of the mission, the broader the range of market and product possibilities; the narrower the scope, the smaller the portfolio of markets and products.

The following case illustrates the usefulness of a business portfolio plan to balance short-term earnings with long-term growth, yet still maintain a competitive advantage.

Westinghouse Electronics Systems

This company has successfully transformed its expertise in surveillance equipment from the defence business to the growing commercial sector.

For Westinghouse, surveillance has a broader strategic direction than just military. Surveillance technology translates into an expansive business portfolio of products and markets, such as electronic products for tracking illegal immigration and drug trafficking, in home security systems, and smart police cars with computer links to government agencies that give immediate analysis of fingerprints.

The plan also identifies profit generating opportunities. It advocates relaunching existing – and paid for – products while avoiding a costly product development period. Thus, revenues were stabilized during the market transition, creating a balance of short-term earnings with long-term growth. With this flexible plan in hand, Westinghouse keeps looking for appropriate market opportunities to expand its business portfolio.

Action strategy

What can you learn from the Westinghouse case?

Effective planning accounts for Westinghouse's smooth transition from defence to commercial markets. With a strategic marketing plan patterned after the format in this chapter, you can achieve short-term goals while preparing for long-term growth. The strategic marketing plan is usually developed with a team of cross-functional personnel from marketing, sales, production, finance, and technical staffs.

Figure 5.2 illustrates how you can construct a workable business portfolio where you can categorize markets and products to reflect your strategic direction. As you view the diagram, note the following structure of the portfolio:

- List existing products into existing markets, the process is identified as *market penetration*.

- Identify existing products for new markets, defined as *market development*.

- Look at introducing new products into existing markets, known as *product development*.

- Indicate new products for new markets, this is expressed as *diversification*.

To use the grid, list products and markets in each of the quadrants. The listing will then serve as a guideline for product-market growth over three to five years.

	Existing products	New products
Existing markets	1. Market penetration	3. Product development
New markets	2. Market development	4. Diversification

Figure 5.2: Business portfolio plan guidelines

Marketing plan: one year

A review of the strategic portion of the SMP makes it apparent that you can no longer think narrowly about a product. Now, you must think about markets within the framework of a tactical marketing plan. The lower rows of boxes in Figure 5.1 make up the tactical marketing plan, which has a timeframe of twelve months. The following overview explains the format and provides a usable perspective.

Situation analysis

The tactical marketing plan begins with a situation analysis of a specific product or market. Whereas the strategic plan looks ahead three to five years, the situation analysis requires that you look back three to five years to obtain an historical perspective of your business.

The situation analysis is divided into three parts:

1. **Marketing mix**. Objectively and factually write your sales and unit volume by product, analyze your pricing, and assess your promotion and distribution.

2. **Market background**. Assess carefully the nature of your audience, buyer behaviour, the image you convey, what customers think about your product, and the frequency of its use.

105

3. **Competitor analysis**. Examine your competitors. Look at their strategies, their products and services, distribution, pricing, and promotional tactics.

Marketing opportunities

After you have analyzed the situation, the next step is to evaluate opportunities. Surprisingly, managers often neglect this part of the process. This planning step is exceedingly important, since the whole purpose of conducting a situation analysis is to expose opportunities.

Opportunities are voids or gaps in a product, a market, or a service that can be filled to satisfy customer needs and wants. This stage of the marketing plan is best achieved by incorporating the input of various functional managers from manufacturing, R&D, product development, finance, and sales.

Brainstorming is a useful technique for identifying opportunities. For example, consider the features and benefits of your product. Study the situation analysis, including your competitive situation, and allow the ideas to flow. Don't attempt to judge them, just record them as they emerge. The probability is that you will discard 90% to 95% of them. But the remaining 5% to 10% could originate the opportunity to enter a new business, form a new product, or render a new service.

Marketing objectives

The third step in the marketing plan is to work out primary and functional marketing objectives. Initially, develop primary quantitative objectives. These include: sales, market share, gross margins, return on investment, return on assets, and any other quantitative information required by your organization.

Next, develop functional objectives. These consist of product, packaging, services, pricing, promotion, and distribution. Such functional areas are commonly referred to as the marketing mix. It should be evident that the marketing mix is a key part of the marketing plan in that it represents the controllable factors you can employ to achieve the primary financial and market objectives.

Strategies and action plans

On the basis of your marketing objectives, you can now develop the strategies and action plans that translate those objectives into action.

Unless you can support your objectives with firm action plans, they are useless. They are no more than good intentions until you develop the strategies and tactics that will make them happen.

Thus, for each objective, develop a strategy and a tactical action plan.

Further, each strategy should include details about what is going to happen, when it is going to happen, and who is responsible for carrying out the action.

Financial controls and budgets

This step in the marketing plan involves the financial controls, budgets, and variance reports that translate into numbers those actions that you have stated in the previous planning steps. Most often, the types of controls and reports usually come from the financial department.

Specifically, however, for tracking marketing and sales performance, you can use these common measurements to measure progress toward achieving your objectives:

- **Current-to-past sales comparisons**. To measure the performance of sales reps and sales territories, you can generate periodic reports on the quantities of products sold by product line, the profitability of territories and any quantitative data specific to measuring the overall selling efficiency of your operation.

- **Customer satisfaction evaluation**. This measure is vitally important when long-term relationship marketing is the strategy of choice. Although a sales representative's likability remains a factor, a more meaningful evaluation should assess outcomes and interests that are important to the customer. These may include being attentive to problems, solving complaints, overcoming technical obstacles, and meeting production schedules.

- **Qualitative evaluation of sales reps**. Use this measure to determine the sales representatives' knowledge of your products, customers, competitors, and territories. Look at the state of the economy and any other issues that would impact the successful outcome of a sale. Also consider evaluating individual characteristics, such as dress, speech and personality as they relate to the image you are trying to reveal to the marketplace.

Best practices

The combination of the three to five year strategic plan and the annual marketing plan form a total strategic marketing plan for use at any level of an organization, from corporate management to product line manager. Further, for every major product and market described in the business portfolio, you should develop a specific annual tactical marketing plan.

In that way, you combine a long-term strategic viewpoint with a one-year tactical framework to create action.

Getting started

1. One of the best approaches to starting your strategic marketing plan is to form a strategy team made up of individuals from different functions of the organization.

2. Involve them to participate totally in the development of the plan, from analyzing the opportunities to creating objectives and strategies.

3. With strategies as the primary output of your strategic marketing plan, use the following checklist to evaluate the practicality of your plan:

   • Are there strategies for enlarging your current markets?

   • Are there strategies for developing new markets?

   • Are there strategies for defining the market and competitive position of the product?

   • Are there strategies for protecting existing sales volume?

   • Are there strategies for launching new products?

6

How to manage your markets: The power of segmentation

Chapter objectives

Segmentation in action

Select a market segment

Eight additonal segment categories to pinpoint markets for greater accuracy

Portfolio analysis

Strength/weakness analysis

Best practices

Chapter objectives

After reading this chapter, you should be able to:

- Employ segmentation techniques to manage your markets.

- Use eight additional segment categories to pinpoint markets for greater accuracy.

- Apply the major screening approaches to evaluate a market segment.

- Conduct a strength/weakness analysis for your business.

Segmentation means splitting the overall market into smaller submarkets or segments that have more in common with one another than with the total market. Subdividing the market helps you identify and satisfy the specific needs of individuals within your selected segments, thereby helping to strengthen your market position. Segmentation also allows you to concentrate your strength against the weaknesses of your competitors, at which point you can improve your competitive ranking.

Segmentation in action

The recent economic boom in several countries of Latin America illustrates how segmentation can work for enterprising managers. This vast region has experienced explosive growth resulting from a variety of dramatic changes, such as: lowering of trade barriers leading to sharp increases in exports, declining inflation and steadier prices, economic recovery and rising incomes, democratic freedom and freer expression, and the profusion of dazzling new communications technologies.

Influenced by these dynamic changes, enterprising managers continue to discover attractive opportunities by segmenting markets and then targeting the identified groups. For example:

- Demographics reveal that of Latin America's nearly half-billion people, almost half the population is younger than 20. Hooked on new technology and yearning to follow the leading trends in world markets, these new consumers hunger for every enticement from fast foods to PC banking.

- With an estimated 35% of women in the workforce, this emerging growth segment is creating a strong demand for new products and services tailored to their individual needs.

- Upgraded telephone lines, the result of privatizing state-run telecom services, have exposed large groups of individuals to the use of the Internet – with the corresponding skyrocketing sales in high-tech products and services.

- With working class Latins grabbing the latest electronic products and with telephone rates and mobile phone prices dropping dramatically, mobile phones are multiplying at triple digit levels, thereby exposing a dynamic and previously overlooked segment.

- Steadier currencies are making it possible for banks to latch on to another emerging segment by offering consumers home mortgages, life insurance, and private pension funds.

- There is a new sensitivity to otherwise poorly served groups, such as the millions of Afro-Latins whose buying power is also rising. Seeing the segment as an opportunity, beauty-products companies are launching a line of make-up to reach this flourishing market. New magazines are also directing editorial attention to satisfying their particular cultural and cosmetic desires.

Identifying a market segment

Accordingly, segmentation works as an integral component in managing your market. Therefore, your ability to accurately concentrate resources in a segment that will yield the greatest payout over the long-term is a skill you need to exploit – if you are to achieve a profitable competitive strategy. For instance, you should know which criteria to use in choosing market segments, what factors to use in identifying a market segment, and how to develop a segmentation analysis.

Use the following criteria to guide you in selecting market segments.

- **Measurable.** Can you quantify the segment? For example, you should be able to quantify how many factories, how many engineers, or how many people with (or without) cellular phones lodge within the market segment.

- **Accessible**. Do you have access to the market through a dedicated salesforce, distributors/dealers, transportation, and the Internet?

- **Substantial**. Is the segment of adequate size to warrant your attention as a viable segment? Further, is the segment declining, maturing, or growing?

111

- **Profitable**. Does concentrating on the segment provide sufficient profitability to make it worthwhile? Use your organization's standard measurements for profitability, such as return on investment, gross margin, or profits.

- **Compatible with competition**. To what extent do your major competitors have an interest in the segment? Is it of active interest or of negligible concern to your competitors?

- **Effectiveness**. Does your organization have acceptable skills and resources to serve the segment effectively?

- **Defendable**. Does your firm have the capabilities to defend itself against the attack of a major competitor?

Answering these questions will help you decide on a market segment with good potential for concentrating your resources, as well as for gaining ample information about your customers and competitors. Once selected, the above criteria can be used to test the feasibility of a market segment. (While new computer software may speed up the segmentation process, be certain the criteria presented here are included when you select the program.)

The following case study provides a more complete perspective of the direct and indirect uses of segmentation.

Ericsson

The Swedish phone giant, Ericsson, operates against a backdrop of intense competition and swift movements in technology. Within that twofold framework, managers face tough decisions about defending their hard-won positions in established segments, determining how to keep ahead of aggressive competitors, and obtaining a foothold in new segments.

For Ericsson, the nagging problem a few years ago was that even with a substantial share of wireless and fixed-line networks, it had lagged in a key telecom growth market: mobile handsets. That void provided hard-driving competitors with an opening to gain solid market positions. For example, Finland's Nokia consolidated its hold on the mobile handset business, with a 23% market share vs. Ericsson's third-place 15%. North American powerhouses such as Cisco Systems and Lucent Technologies also seized the lead in the Internet telephony field.

Ericsson's strategy

To fight back, the Stockholm-based company took the following steps:

1. Recognizing a prime opportunity, Ericsson employed its vast technical expertise to concentrate heavily on the growing applications for mobile phones to transmit reams of information.

2. The company also expanded the market for mobile phones by intensifying its efforts to offer wireless Internet access.

3. As the wireless networks multiplied, Ericsson managers focused on the remarkable growth forecasts for mobile subscribers worldwide. Based on those healthy projections for the forseeable future, Ericsson also saw a massive market for equipment upgrades and thereby positioned itself to grab a significant piece of that market segment.

Strategy lessons

If you have responsibility for budgeting company resources responsibly and strategically, the Ericsson case highlights the following strategy lessons:

1. Divide your market into viable segments that conform to your company's growth plans, and which offer you a sustainable competitive advantage.

2. Employ a reliable and systematic procedure called portfolio analysis (described later in this chapter) to screen and exploit segment opportunities.

Let's first examine the approaches to dividing your market into meaningful segments.

Select a market segment

Figure 6.1 displays the four most common ways to segment a market, based on demographic, geographic, psychographic, and product attribute factors. Each of these approaches, singly or in combination with the others, represent an opportunity that can be satisfied with a product or service.

Demographic segmentation	Psychographic segmentation
Sex	Life styles
Age	
Family life cycle	Psychological variables:
Race/ethnic group	– Personality
Education	– Self-image
Income	– Cultural influences
Occupation	
Family size	
Religion	
Home ownership	
Geographic segmentation	**Product attribute segmentation**

Figure 6.1: Bases for market segmentation

To apply market segmentation to your strategy, you need a thorough understanding of the various categories of segments. Let's examine the following most common approaches to segmenting a market: demographic, geographic, psychographic, and product attributes.

Demographic segmentation

Demographic variables are among the most widely used segmentation approaches. They owe their popularity to two facts:

1. They are easier to observe and/or measure than most other characteristics.

2. Their breakdown of sex, age, family life cycle, race/ethnic group, education, income, occupation, family size, religion, and home ownership are often closely linked to differences in behavioural patterns.

In many instances, you can combine demographic variables to produce a more meaningful breakdown rather than relying on a single criterion. For example, it is common to combine the age of the head of the household with the family size and the level of household income.

If four age levels, three family sizes, and three income levels are distinguished, a total of 36 segments result. Using a combination of primary data, secondary data, and judgment, you can then determine the value of each segment and thus arrive at a well-thought-out conclusion about which segments warrant your efforts.

Watch out, however, for unrelated demographic characteristics that could be unreliable: gender may produce marginal differences in the usage patterns of telephones or in the consumption of toothpaste and soft drinks. Chronological age is also not always a reliable indicator of behavioural patterns and income level may prove relevant only when used with other variables such as social class, family life cycle, and occupation.

Geographic segmentation

Geographic segmentation is relatively easy to perform because the individual segments can be clearly defined on a map. It is a sensible strategy to employ when there are distinct differences in climatic conditions, access to transportation, proximity to round-the-clock service or repairs – as well as with such geographic considerations as varying regional tastes or unique culture-based habits and behaviours.

Geographic segmentation even extends to facial features used in advertising. When Kodak introduced its original Instamatic camera worldwide, the company quickly learned through adverse market feedback that potential consumers in many countries around the globe, from the Philippines to India and from Hong Kong to South Africa, could not relate to the Caucasian girl portrayed in the advertising. Kodak promptly modified its advertising by using local models and this contributed to a phenomenal success story.

Internationally, blocks or clusters of countries can often be approached in a similar fashion, particularly if they share the same language and cultural heritage. For instance, in most of Latin America the same advertising media are often appropriate for several countries.

While there are numerous cultural differences in many of those countries – as well as in other parts of the world – there are common problems with shared features. Known as cultural universals, these commonalties include economic systems, marriage and family systems, educational systems, social control systems, and supernatural belief systems.

Geographically, you can segment by region, city size, population density, or by geopolictical criteria. However, such segmentation is effective only if it reflects differences in need and buying patterns. Many firms, for example, adjust their advertising efforts to as small an area as a county.

Psychographic segmentation

The most exciting form of segmentation results from the application of psychographic variables, such as life style, personality, and self image. Banks, car manufacturers, and liquor producers, to name a few, benefit from the advantages of psychographic segmentation. It is a branch of market segmentation that continues to evolve and promises great vitality in the future.

Department stores use lifestyle departments that vary according to neighbourhoods. However, personality is still an isolated psychographic variable and requires developmental work before it can prove a valid criterion for segmentation.

Overall, the next wave of psychographic inquiry would benefit greatly with the active involvement of cultural anthropologists. Building on their collective expertise, they can delve into the behavioural patterns, mannerisms, and rules of conduct displayed by target groups. In turn, these experts can offer their insight and direction to business managers for use in serving the best interests of consumers.

Product attributes

Product attributes include usage rates defined as: non-user, ex-user, potential user, first-time user, and regular user groups.

In practice, such information is further broken down to distinguish non-users, light, medium, and heavy users of a product. Often, heavy users of a product represent a relatively small share of total consumer or business buyers; yet they account for the major portion of the sales volume in the market. These breakdowns, in turn, would trigger different motivational appeals to improve the level of responsiveness from various segments.

In other applications, companies with high market share might be especially eager to monitor their position in a given market segment, while smaller competitors with lower market share would devote their efforts to converting new users to their brand.

Overall, you will find product attributes most practical in segmenting a market, and particularly applicable in deciding where to deploy a salesforce, allocate budgets, prioritize product development projects, and direct promotional campaigns for maximum impact.

Eight additonal segment categories to pinpoint markets for greater accuracy

To provide a more comprehensive approach to selecting market segments and for determining your optimum marketing strategy, classify them using the following additional segment categories: *natural, leading edge, key, linked, central, challenging, difficult,* and *encircled.*

Using these eight categories as a guide, you can look with a more critical eye at what challenges you will face. Then you will be better able to assess the risks and potential rewards as you make your selection. The emphasis on these segment categories is marketing strategy.

As you examine the characteristics for each segment category, you may find some overlapping. That is acceptable since there are common traits that are innate among the various markets.

Natural segments

Here a company operates in the familiar setting of its normal or traditional market segment. The inference is that within such customary surroundings, personnel tend to be at ease and generally are not motivated to venture out of their comfort zone. To expand, they have to be motivated to move beyond the confines of existing segments. Also, does your organization's strategic goals permit venturing out of familiar territory?

For the most part, you and your rivals can operate harmoniously within the broader market. That condition exits as long as each company sticks to its own dedicated segment. Generally, outright aggressive confrontations are seldom used.

The primary reason for this uncharacteristic display of togetherness in a competitive world is that you and your rivals share a common interest in furthering the long-term growth and prosperity of the market as a whole.

If any one company chooses to gain a meaningful benefit, a likely strategy might include securing a more advantageous position on the supply chain. Or it could mean adjusting its position by adding or

117

deleting a link in the distribution chain. Doing so would be sufficient to differentiate one company from a competitor and permit it to meet unfolding supply and demand situations with greater efficiency.

Even with the mayhem of global rivals scrambling for market share, or price wars eating away at profitability, it is still possible to have some semblance of market unity in natural markets.

There is one additional dimension that characterizes this segment, which you should actively keep in the forefront of your thinking: Industries, markets, and products go through successive life cycle stages from introduction, growth, maturity, decline, to phase-out.

Much of the movement through those stages is driven by the adoption rate of technology, which precedes or follows changes in consumer behaviour. There are also external changes triggered by legislative or environmental factors generally out of a manager's ability to control.

Therefore, to maintain growth, take the lead in uncovering new niches within the segment. Doing so also provides the impetus that drives new product development.

Leading edge segments

Leading edge means exploring segments by making minor penetrations into a competitor's territory. The intent is to investigate the possibility of opening another revenue stream.

Therefore, you want to acquire the following types of intelligence:

1. the feasibility of the market to generate revenue over the long term,

2. the amount of investment needed to enter and gain a foothold in the segment,

3. the timeframe for payback and eventual profitability, and

4. an assessment of competitors' market position and strengths/ weaknesses.

A now classic example of a leading edge market is the initial penetration by a few Japanese companies into the North American market with small copiers. Xerox, the market leader during the 1970s, concentrated its marketing efforts to large corporations with a line of large copiers.

Xerox managers initially avoided the small copier market. That oversight proved to be a critical error: It allowed enterprising Japanese copier makers to exploit a wide-open opportunity to walk unopposed into the vast market of small and mid-size firms. Once established, they moved upscale in a segment-by-segment assault and took over a significant amount of Xerox's primary market share.

Key segments

Key means that you and many of your competitors seem evenly matched within key market segments. The general behaviour is that you would not openly oppose an equally strong rival.

However, should a competitor attempt an attack against your long-held position with the clear aim of taking away customers or disrupting your supply chain relationships, then you are forced to launch a counter effort by concentrating as many resources to blunt the effort. Such actions are appropriate, however, if they fit your overall strategic objectives.

Therefore, keep the strategic big picture in mind: If you expend excessive resources in hawkish-style actions such as price wars, then you may be left with a restricted budget to defend your market position.

Linked segments

In this category, you and your competitors are linked with easy access to markets. Your best strategy is to pay strict attention to constructing barriers around those niches that you value most, and from which you can best defend your position.

Barriers include:

- Above-average quality
- Feature-loaded products
- First-class customer service
- Superior technical support
- Competitive pricing
- On-time delivery
- Generous warranties
- Patent protection

Not only do they build barriers against competitors' incursions, they also go a long way in solidifying customer loyalty. In particular, customer loyalty gives you a long-lasting, profit-generating advantage that is difficult for a competitor to overcome. It is the one area that makes a meaningful addition to your growth.

Central segments

Central means that a company faces powerful forces that threaten its superior market position. These forces are as diverse as watching small companies niche away at a market leader's position through aggressive pricing; or observing others offering dazzling feature-laden products; or looking at technology-rich firms generating new applications overlaid with enhanced value-added services.

To counter such threats, firms use joint ventures so that the cumulative effects yield greater market advantages and strategy options than can be achieved independently. For many companies the merger and acquisition (M&A) route and other forms of joint ventures have proven the strategy of choice.

Challenging segments

In this category, if you enter a segment dominated by a strong and aggressive competitor, be watchful. You could place your company at excessively high risk.

If, however, your long-term objectives strongly support maintaining a presence in a challenging market, and if the expenditures of financial, material, and human resources are consistent with your overall strategy, then find a secure position on the supply chain. It could be one of your single best chances for lessening the risk and achieving a solid measure of success. Your intent is to rely on efficient distribution to ensure the movement of finished products to customers.

Difficult segments

This type of segment is characterized as one where progress is particularly slow and labour intensive. If attempting to make any meaningful market penetration, secure key accounts, or maintain reasonable levels of logistical support, you are likely to be blocked by asset-draining barriers.

Overall, meagre revenues and high costs typify this type of segment. Your best strategy is to go forward with your marketing efforts, as long as they are consistent with your mission and long-term strategic objectives.

Your starting point: Develop a strategic marketing plan, as described in Chapter 5. It represents one of the key decision-making formats for developing objectives and strategies.

In its most pragmatic usage, the plan serves as a laser-focused beacon to prevent you from wandering off and following every Monday morning headline, which often results in diverting your efforts and squandering resources into segments unsuitable to your company.

Encircled segments

Encircled foretells a potentially risky situation. This market condition exists when you control limited resources and any aggressive action by a competitor can force you to consider pulling out of a segment.

Therefore, it is in your best interest to maintain ongoing competitive intelligence to accurately assess the vulnerability of your position against that of your opponent.

Armed with the intelligence, you can then develop a contingency plan that highlights your strengths and exposes your competitor's weaknesses. If in your judgment, you still lack manoeuverability and a capability to mount a meaningful competitive response, then exiting the segment is a prudent way out, as long as it minimizes disruption to your main line of business.

If, on the other hand, your competitor foresees an untenable position, it is wise to give the rival a way out of the market and not force him into a fight-to-the-end mindset.

Strategies include:

1. Exploit a competitor's weaknesses and aggressively stay ahead by developing product enhancements.

2. Launch value-added services.

3. Initiate any other programs that would hamper his ability to maintain a profitable market position.

The aim of the psychological-based strategy is to discourage your opponent from making a monumental effort to survive. Instead, encourage him to take the more tempting approach and exit the market. To implement the three-part strategy, it is best to form cross-functional teams.

Portfolio analysis

Referring again to the Ericsson case, another lesson becomes apparent: It calls for the use of a reliable and systematic procedure called portfolio analysis to help in selecting segments.

Portfolio analysis consists of formal models that use a variety of key criteria to rate the attractiveness of markets. In practice, portfolio analysis is an excellent quantitative tool for use by all size firms to make investment decisions on a market-by-market or product-by-product basis.

Your job, therefore, is to assemble the essential information for these portfolio approaches and decide on which model suits your business. The results can provide immeasurable help in systematically selecting a market segment, analyzing your competitive situation, and developing marketing strategies.

The following case introduces you to the practical application of portfolio analysis.

Imperial Chemical Industries

This company has traditionally served the bulk chemicals market. However, for the last several years that market suffered from intense competition, a downturn in the economy, a strong sterling pound, and the fall of commodity prices.

Addressing the potentially dangerous situation that would send the company into a spiral, ICI management began activating the following business-building strategies to reverse the situation and regain its traditional long-term pathway for growth.

ICI's strategies

- Spend heavily on strengthening its line of speciality products such as flavours and fragrances; industrial adhesives, starches, and paints. ICI also broadened its product base through acquisitions. It purchased two leading U.S.-based companies: National Starch & Chemical Co., a leader in supplying adhesives that companies such as Intel Corp. use in assembling packages of chips; the other was Quest which produces fragrances and is involved in the profitable business of creating new flavours and textures for foods.

- Sell off significant portions of its bulk chemical businesses including natural and synthetic lubricants and personal care products. ICI management also concluded after studying the competitive situation that it no longer had the marketing power to compete with the industry leaders in bulk chemicals.

- Shift sales emphasis from Britain to Continental Europe and North America. By acquiring strong companies both in the U.S. and on the Continent, ICI established an immediate presence in those lucrative markets. ICI also moved into specialized regional and industrial segments by marketing explosives, soda ash, sulphur-related products, and fibres.

In implementing these strategies and managing such a diverse portfolio of products and market segments, ICI management exercised meticulous judgment in specifying which companies to buy and those to sell, and which markets to build, maintain, or exit.

The following section describes three of the more popular models of portfolio analysis used in assessing markets and products, all of which can apply to your business: BCG growth-share matrix, General Electric business screen, and the Arthur D. Little matrix.

BCG growth-share matrix

With a technique developed by the Boston Consulting Group, this classic model can prove highly useful in assessing a portfolio of businesses or products. The BCG growth-share matrix (Figure 6.2) graphically shows that some products may enjoy a strong position relative to those of competitors, while other products languish in a weaker position.

As such, each product benefits from a distinct strategy depending on its position in the matrix. The various circles represent a product. From the positioning of these circles, management can determine the following information:

- Monetary sales, represented by the area of the circle.

- Market share, relative to the firm's largest competitor, as shown by the horizontal position.

- Growth rate, relative to the market in which the product competes, as shown by the vertical position.

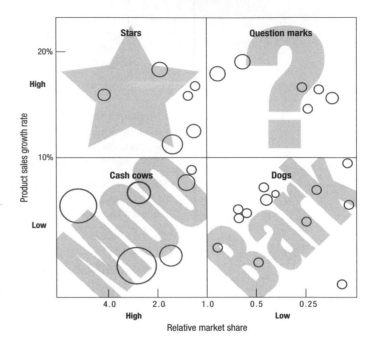

Figure 6.2: BCG growth-share matrix

In addition, the quadrants of the matrix arrange products into four groups:

1. **Stars**: products that have high market growth and high market share. These products need constant attention to maintain or increase share through active promotion, effective distribution coverage, product improvement, and careful pricing strategies.

2. **Cash cows**: products that have low market growth and high market share. Such products usually hold market dominance and generate strong cash flow. The object: retain a strong market presence without large expenditures for promotion and with minimal outlay for R&D. The central idea behind the cash cow is that businesses with a large share of the market are more profitable than their smaller-share competitors.

3. **Question marks** (also known as problem children or wild-cats): products with potential for high growth in a fast-moving market but with low market share. They absorb large amounts

of cash (usually taken from the cash cows) and are expected to eventually reach the status of a star.

4. **Dogs**: products with low market growth and low market share, reflecting the worst of all situations. A number of alternatives are possible: maintain the product in the line to support the image of a full-line supplier and thereby deny access to the market through which an eager competitor could enter, quickly eliminate the product from the line, or harvest the product through a slow phase out.

As you review the growth-share matrix, note on the vertical axis how product sales are separated into high and low quadrants. The 10% growth line is simply an arbitrary rate of growth and represents a middle level. For your particular industry the number could be 5%, 12%, or 15%.

Similarly, on the horizontal axis there is a dividing line of relative market share of 1.0 so that positioning your product in the lower left-hand quadrant would indicate high market leadership, and in the lower right-hand quadrant, low market leadership.

The significant interpretations of the matrix are as follows:

- The amount of cash generated increases with relative market share.

- The amount of sales growth requires proportional cash input to finance the added capacity for market development. If market share is maintained, then cash requirements increase only relative to market growth rate.

- Increases in market share usually require cash to support advertising and sales promotion expenditures, lower prices, and other share-building tactics. On the other hand, a decrease in market share may provide cash for use in other product areas.

- Where a product moves towards maturity, it is possible to use just enough funds to maintain market position and use surplus funds to reinvest in other products that are still growing.

In summary, the BCG growth-share matrix permits you to evaluate where your products and markets are, relative to competitors. It also helps you calculate what investments are needed to support such basic strategies as expanding into emerging market segments, building share for your product in existing markets, harvesting products, or withdrawing from the market.

General Electric business screen

The BCG growth-share matrix focuses on cash flow and uses only two variables: growth and market share. On the other hand, the General Electric business screen (Figure 6.3), also known as multi-factor analysis, is a more comprehensive analysis that provides a graphic display of where an existing product fits competitively in relation to a variety of criteria. It also aids in projecting the chances for a new product's success.

The key points in using the GE business screen:

1. *Industry attractiveness* is shown on the vertical axis of the matrix. It is based on rating such factors as market size, market growth rate, profit margin, competitive intensity, cyclicality, seasonality, and scale of economies. Each factor is then given a weight of high, medium, or low in overall attractiveness to classify an industry, market segment, or product.

2. *Business strength* is shown on the horizontal axis of the matrix. A weighted rating is made for such factors as relative market share, price competitiveness, product quality, knowledge of customer and market, sales effectiveness, and geography. The results show your ability to compete and, in turn, provide insight into developing strategies in relation to competitors.

3. The matrix is divided into three-colour sectors: green, yellow, and red. The green sector has three cells at the upper left and indicates those markets that are favourable in industry attractiveness and business strength. These markets have a 'green light' to move in aggressively. The yellow sector includes the diagonal cells stretching from the lower left to upper right. This sector indicates a medium level in overall attractiveness. The red sector covers the three cells in the lower right. This sector indicates those markets that are low in overall attractiveness.

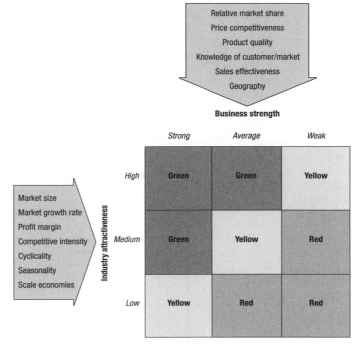

Figure 6.3: General Electric business screen

A more comprehensive view of the factors contributing to industry attractiveness and business strength is given in Table 6.1. The variety of factors is not meant to overwhelm you, but to provide for the practical application of any factors that could possibly contribute to a more meaningful analysis. For your personal use, you can add or delete factors to suit your business and industry.

Market attractiveness	
Market size	Measures size of key segments, your share of each segment relative to closest competitors
Market growth rate	Identifies annual rate of growth projected over a three to five year period
Profit margins	Indicates your margins and relationship of margins to your company's financial criteria
Competitive intensity	Compares types of competitors in terms of products, pricing, distribution, promotion, personnel, marketing capability, market share by segment and competitor
Cyclicality, seasonality	Determines effects of economic, industry, technology, or seasonality cycles on segment entry and growth rate
Scale economies	Measures effects of economies of scale and experience related to productivity and profitability
Business strength	
Relative market share	Compares competitors within an overall market, individual segments, product applications, and against top three competitors
Price competitiveness	Sensitivity to price, value-added services, offerings of competitors, external market factors
Product quality	Measures customer perceptions of quality, price/value relationships, comparisons with competitors' offerings
Knowledge of customer/market	Indicates level of market intelligence related to how business will change in three to five years; customer functions to be satisfied as market evolves; technologies needed to satisfy customer/ market needs; changes anticipated in buyer behaviour, competition, environment, culture, and the economy
Sales effectiveness	Evaluates efficiency of sales force, advertising, sales promotion; weighs impact of the Internet on sales force functions and distribution channels
Geography	Assesses movement of key customers, changes in location of selected segments, ability to provide adequate market coverage and service

Table 6.1. Factors contributing to market attractiveness and business strength

Finally, to show an even more practical application of the GE business screen, Figure 6.4 illustrates the strategy options for each of the nine cells of the matrix.

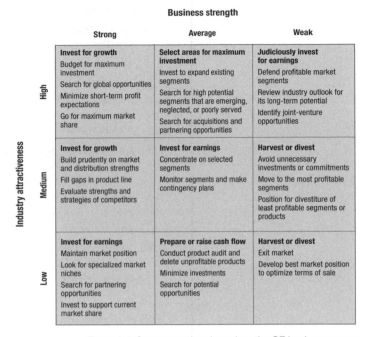

Figure 6.4: Strategy options based on the GE business screen

Arthur D. Little matrix

Another time-tested portfolio analysis approach is associated with the consulting organization, Arthur D. Little Inc. In one actual application, a major manufacturer in the health care industry used this approach to analyze how its various products stacked up in market share.

In Figure 6.5, some of the company's products are used to demonstrate the function of this matrix. First, note the similarities of this format to the other portfolio analysis approaches already discussed.

The competitive positions of various products are plotted on the vertical axis according to such factors as leading, strong, favourable, tenable, weak, and non-viable. On the horizontal axis, the maturity levels for the products are designated embryonic, growth, mature, and aging.

The key interpretations for this matrix are:

1. **Non-viable**: indicates the lowest possible level of competitive position.

2. **Weak**: designates unsatisfactory financial performance but with some opportunity for improvement.

3. **Tenable**: shows a competitive product position where financial performance is barely satisfactory. These products have a less than average opportunity to improve competitive position.

4. **Favourable**: displays a competitive position that is better than the survival rate. These products also have a limited range of opportunities for improvement.

5. **Strong**: suggests an ability to defend market share against competing moves without the sacrifice of acceptable financial performance.

6. **Leading**: reveals the widest range of strategic options because of the competitive distance between the given products and the competitors' products.

An examination of the four products shows how this matrix worked during a particular period in those products' life cycle.

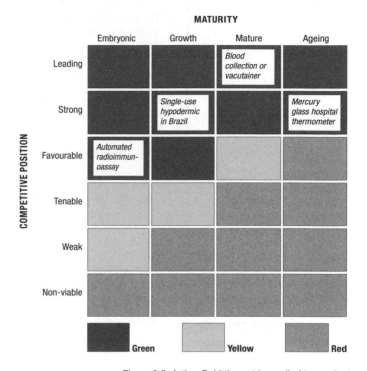

Figure 6.5: Arthur D. Little matrix applied to products

Automated radioimmunoassay (a sophisticated diagnostic product used in laboratories) was considered in its embryonic stage with a favourable competitive position at the time the analysis was prepared. This favourable position offered the manager a range of strategy options, as long as the decisions related to the overall corporate strategy.

Single-use hypodermic needles and syringes had a strong competitive position in a growth industry. Here, too, strategy options were fairly flexible and depended on competitive moves as well as on how quickly increases in market share were desired.

A blood collection system (vacutainers) had a leading competitive position in a mature industry. To hold existing market share, the company's strategy centred on product differentiation.

Mercury glass hospital thermometers had a strong competitive position in a declining industry. This product had less price flexibility. However, by using service, repackaging, and distribution innovations, the company attempted to maintain its strong position before giving in to price reductions.

As in the GE business screen, a green-yellow-red system is used to indicate strategic options. Green indicates a wide range of options; yellow indicates caution for a limited range of options for selected development; and red is a warning of peril with options narrowed to those of withdrawal, divestiture, and liquidation.

The three major screening tools described above can add greater precision to your decisions and aid you in allocating resources to market segments and products for the greatest return.

One final approach to managing your business and markets is to assess your company's capabilities. It is the definitive technique as you make the hard decisions to pursue, retain, or defend markets. The approach is to conduct a comprehensive strength/weakness analysis. You can use the 100-question checklist that follows as it is, or modify the questions to suit your industry and business.

Strength/ weakness analysis

The strengths/weaknesses analysis questionnaire, Figure 6.6, consists of 100 questions and serves as a marketing audit in two ways:

1. You analyze marketing operations and key external factors affecting your company.

2. You assess your company's internal competencies and strategic marketing capabilities and determine what strategies can be used to increase competitive advantage.

The analysis itself consists of three parts:

1. It analyzes the *overall marketing environment* in which your firm operates. By looking at such domains as consumers (end-use buyers), customers (intermediate buyers), competitors, and environmental (political, legal, technological), you can create a picture of major forces shaping your business situation.

2. It reviews *marketing management procedures* and policies in areas such as analysis, planning, implementation and control, and organization. This review focuses on the internal workings of your organization so you can assess competitive fitness.

3. It examines strategy aspects of the *marketing mix* by considering how you handle your product, pricing, promotion, and distribution. This third part is a good integration of the way your organization is responding to external forces and provides a test of your company's capabilities to respond to the environment and a market orientation.

For best results, form a task-force to provide objective answers to the questions. Some organizations obtain excellent results by calling in a knowledgeable consultant to work with the task-force. If you can keep in mind that the purpose of this time-consuming analysis is to develop competitive strategies and thereby create competitive advantage, perhaps you can justify the labour-intensive task.

PART 1: REVIEWING YOUR FIRM'S MARKETING ENVIRONMENT

Consumers

1. Who are your ultimate buyers?
2. Who or what influences them in their buying decisions?
3. What are you consumers' demographic and psychographic profiles?
4. When, where, and how do they shop for and consume your product?
5. What need(s) does your product satisfy?
6. How well does it satisfy?
7. How can you best segment your target market?
8. How do prospective buyers perceive your product in their minds?
9. What are the economic conditions and expectations of your target market?
10. Are your consumers' attitudes, values, or habits changing?

Customers

11. Who are your customers – that is, intermediate buyers (wholesalers and/or retailers)?
12. Who or what influences them in their buying decisions?
13. Where are your customers located?
14. What other products do they carry?
15. What is their size, and what percentage of your total revenue does each group represent?
16. How well do they serve your target market?
17. How well do you serve their needs?
18. How much support do they give your product?
19. What made you select them and them select you?
20. How can you motivate them to work harder for you?
21. Do you need them?
22. Do they need you?
23. Do you use multiple channels?
24. Would you be better off setting up your own distribution system?
25. Should you go direct?

Customers *(continued)*

26. Who are your competitors?

27. Where are they located?

28. How big are they overall and, specifically, in your product area?

29. What is their product mix?

30. Is their participation in this field growing or declining?

31. Which competitors may be leaving the field?

32. What new domestic competitors may be on the horizon?

33. What new international competitors may be on the horizon?

34. Which competitive strategies and tactics appear particularly successful or unsuccessful?

35. What new directions is the competition pursuing?

Other relevant environmental components

36. What are the legal constraints affecting your marketing effort?

37. To what extent does government regulation restrict your flexibility in making marketing decisions?

38. What requirements do you have to meet?

39. What political or legal developments are looming that will improve or worsen your situation?

40. What threats or opportunities does technological progress hold in store for you?

41. How well do you keep up with technology in the lab and in the plant?

42. What broad cultural shifts are occurring that may affect your business?

43. What consequences will demographic and geographic shifts have for your business?

44. Are any changes in resource availability foreseeable?

45. How do you propose to cope with ecological constraints?

PART II: REVIEWING MARKETING MANAGEMENT PROCEDURES AND POLICIES

Analysis

46. Do you have an established marketing research function?
47. Do you conduct regular and systematic market analyses?
48. Do you subscribe to any regular market data service?
49. Do you test and retest carefully before you introduce a new product?
50. Are all your major marketing decisions based on solidly researched facts?

Planning

51. How carefully do you examine and how aggressively do you cope with problems, difficulties, challenges, and threats to your business?
52. How do you identify and capitalize on opportunities in your marketplace?
53. What care is given in determining major gaps in needs?
54. Do you develop clearly stated and prioritized short-term and long-term marketing objectives?
55. What are your marketing objectives?
56. Are your marketing objectives achievable and measurable?
57. Do you have a formalized annual marketing planning procedure?
58. Do you manage by objectives?
59. What is your core strategy for achieving your marketing objectives?
60. Are you employing a push (through intermediaries) or pull (through consumers) as a marketing strategy?
61. How aggressively are you considering or employing diversification?
62. How effectively are you segmenting your target market?
63. Are you allocating sufficient or excessive marketing resources to accomplish your marketing tasks?
64. Are your marketing resources optimally allocated to the major elements of your marketing mix?
65. How well do you tie in your marketing plan with the other functional plans of your organization?

Implementation and control

66. Is your marketing plan truly followed or just filed away?
67. Do you continuously monitor your environment to determine the adequacy of your plan?
68. Do you use control mechanisms to ensure achievement of your objectives?
69. Do you compare planned to actual figures periodically and take appropriate measures if they differ significantly?
70. Do you systematically study the contribution and effectiveness of various marketing activities?

Organization

71. Does your firm have a high-level marketing office to analyze, plan, and oversee the implementation of your marketing effort?

72. How capable and dedicated are your marketing personnel?

73. Is there a need for more training, incentives, supervision, or evaluation?

74. Are your marketing responsibilities structured to best serve the needs of different marketing activities, products, target markets, and sales territories?

75. Does your entire organization embrace and practise relationship marketing with a total customer-driven orientation?

PART III: REVIEWING STRATEGY ASPECTS OF THE MARKETING MIX

Product policy

76. What is the make-up of your product mix and how well are its components selling?

77. Does it have optimal breadth and depth?

78. Should any of your products be phased out?

79. Do you carefully evaluate any negative ripple effects on the remaining product mix before you make a decision to phase out a product?

80. Have you considered modification, repositioning, and/or extension of sagging products?

81. What additions, if any, should be made to your product mix?

82. Which products are you best equipped to make yourselves and which items should you buy and resell under your own company or brand name?

83. Do you routinely check product safety and product liability?

84. Do you have a formalized and tested product recall procedure?

85. Is any recall imminent?

Pricing

86. To what degree are your prices based on cost, demand, and/or competitive considerations?

87. How would your customers react to higher or lower prices?

88. Do you use temporary price promotions and, if so, how effective are they?

89. Do you suggest resale prices?

90. How do your wholesale or retail margins and discounts compare with those of the competition?

Promotion
91. Do you state your advertising objectives clearly?
92. Do you spend enough, too much, or too little on advertising?
93. Are your advertising copy themes effective?
94. Is your media mix optimal and have you assessed the potential of the Internet?
95. Do you make aggressive use of sales promotion techniques?
Personal selling and distribution
96. Is your salesforce at the right strength to accomplish your marketing objectives and to what extent will the Internet affect your salesforce?
97. Is it optimally organized according to geographic, market, or product criteria?
98. Is it adequately trained and motivated, and characterized by high morale, ability, and effectiveness?
99. Have you optimized your distribution setup, or are there opportunities for further streamlining?
100. Is your customer service meeting the needs of your customers?

Figure 6.6: Strengths/weaknesses analysis

Best practices

1. Search for opportunities in unserved, poorly served, or emerging market segments. When identified, selectively penetrate and expand the most promising niches by improving products and services, stretching product lines, and positioning your product to the needs of customers and against competitors.

2. Identify ways to create new opportunities in segments by participating in promising new technologies and innovations. Along with others in your group, try to pioneer something new or unique.

3. Monitor changing behavioural patterns and preferences. For instance, practise segmenting a market according to evolving purchasing patterns, such as through the Internet. Also, identify clusters of customers who might buy or utilize different services for different reasons.

4. Learn how your competitors segment their markets; what products and services they offer; what strategies they pursue; and how they promote, distribute, and price.

7

How to manage your product strategy

Chapter objectives

Product life cycle

Product competition

Product mix

Product design

New products/ services

Product audit

Best practices

Chapter objectives

After reading this chapter, you should be able to:

- Use a framework consisting of six major factors to develop product strategies.

- Employ product life cycle guidelines to revitalize sales and extend the life of your products.

- Define the four-phase process for developing a new product.

- Use the product audit to sustain product profitability.

- Convert product strategies into action.

As you review your products or services, you are presented with a dual opportunity. First, you tend to become mindful of the changing needs and wants of customers, the life-line to successful new product development. Second, you incline towards a more prudent path in deciding how and when to remove losing and marginal products.

The six major areas of product considerations – product life cycle, product competition, product mix, product design, new products, and product audit – provide a systematic framework for reviewing your products and developing competitive strategies.

The following case shows how one company devised strategies to revitalize its product line and prevent it from becoming an also-ran in the industry.

Timex

The well-known watchmaker, Timex, is an inspiring example for those managers who must reconfigure their product lines weakened by aggressive competition, management mistakes, and changing market behaviour.

Let's look at the conditions that hit Timex and then examine their strategies. Management's errors were few but potent. In the early 1980s, a Swiss company asked Timex to handle worldwide marketing of its new line of watches. Management refused and the Swatch went on to become one of that decade's immensely successful products.

When competitors, particularly Japanese makers, latched on to Texas Instrument's invention of the digital watch that swept the market during the 1970s and 1980s, Timex elected to stick with conventional, low-priced analogue watches.

At the same time, consumer behaviour was changing. Timepieces became fashion accessories, not just functional objects. Statistics revealed the average consumer owned five watches, compared with one-and-a-half 30 years earlier.

Aggressive competitors such as Seiko and Citizen spotted the trend and rushed in with a wide variety of styles in a growing price range. Again, Timex remained conservative, even while its market share nose-dived.

So much for the errors. How did Timex management reposition itself, build its product line, and salvage a valuable brand name?

Timex's strategies

- **Market orientation**. Recognizing its errors, management moved rapidly to obtain first-hand market feedback to drive new product development. Fashion consultants from New York and Paris visited Timex's headquarters regularly to display new clothing styles and suggest trends that could influence watch styles.

- **Product expansion**. Timex began making watches for Guess and Versace, under license. The company thereby moved into upscale markets and with a fresh and expanded product lineup. A deal with Nautica Apparel introduced the first dress watch for men, movie characters were licensed from Disney for a new product line, and Timex licensed its own name for a line of wall clocks and clock radios.

- **Product development**. Timex's biggest product coup occurred with the launch of its Indiglo line. Using a patented technology, energy comes from the watch batteries to excite electrons that light up the watch face. (The brightness of its Indiglo watch helped a man lead a group of people down 34 flights of dark stairs after the first World Trade centre bombing.) Then, remembering the Swatch incident, Timex developed a plastic line called Watercolours to go up against their Swiss rival. Also, noticing the sports craze, Timex moved rapidly with the highly successful Ironman to capture a big share of that growth segment. Then, new product development charged forward into high-tech items capable of paging or downloading computer data.

- **Organizational restructuring**. Management learned the hard way that becoming aware of market changes and responding quickly with products at the right time and place are the ingredients for successful repositioning. Accordingly, the privately-owned company reorganized along product lines, creating business units for sport, fashion, and its core Timex watches, giving each line full autonomy over product design and development.

Action strategy

What can you learn from the Timex case? Timex's strategies are instructive as you consider the broader considerations of product strategy. Use the following guidelines:

1. **Keep focused**. Position your products in those niches where there is an above average chance to rank favourably among the industry leaders. Where possible, avoid the commodity segments where price becomes the central competitive issue. Instead, find a technology, product design, distribution system, or value-added service that differentiates your products from those of your competitors.

2. **Establish flexible work teams**. The traditional organizational hierarchy is gone. Cross-functional teams now create the vital linkage between customers and successful product strategies. To implement the action, the team must have the authority to make decisions and team members should be properly trained in the techniques of developing strategic marketing plans that include product strategies.

3. **Solve customers' problems**. The extent to which you are able to solve customers' problems and thereby make your customers more competitive, the greater chance you have for survival and long-term growth. In solving customers' problems, search for new product applications, develop value-added services, and explore new market segments that were overlooked in the initial stages of product development.

4. **Look globally**. Trade barriers continue to crumble. Push your product ideas and technologies wherever they apply in the world. However, follow the principles indicated above. That is, make sure you are positioned to offer a speciality or customized product that will satisfy local needs, and not use foreign markets as a means to unload a standardized product.

Product life cycle

Revitalizing sales

Overview: The various strategies that extend the sales life of products are the pillars for successful growth (Figure 7.1). These life cycle extenders are the safest and most economical strategies to follow. First, identify the best extension opportunities. Then gain the cooperation of product developers, manufacturing, finance, distribution, marketing, and sales.

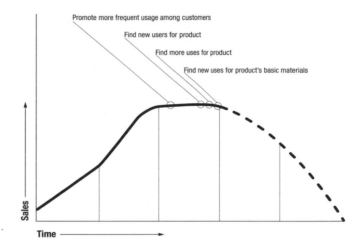

Promote more frequent usage among customers

Find new users for product

Find more uses for product

Find new uses for product's basic materials

Sales

Time

Figure 7.1: Strategy application for extending a product's life cycle

Examples

Examples abound of organizations successfully extending the sales life of their products. The classics include nylon, Jell-O brand gelatin desserts, and Scotch brand tape. All have had average life cycles of more than 70 years and are still going strong.

DuPont nylon was used initially for parachutes in World War II. Then the social necessity for women to wear hosiery promoted the use of nylon. It was also introduced in a variety of textures and colours and its use extended to rugs, tyres, clothing, and a variety of applications in the consumer and industrial markets.

Jell-O expanded its assortment of flavours and promoted the product for use in salads as well as deserts. It also focused on the weight-watching market.

3M introduced Scotch brand tape in a variety of tape dispensers to encourage more usage. It developed coloured, patterned, waterproof, and write-on tape. It also developed new uses for the basic material with double-coated tapes that competed with liquid adhesives for industrial applications.

Thus, the product life cycle offers you a reliable perspective for observing – and influencing – a 'living' product moving through dynamic stages.

Consequently, the classic product life cycle model remains an effective framework for devising marketing strategies at various stages of the curve.

Strategies throughout the life cycle

Different conditions characterize the stages of the product life cycle, influenced by outside economic, social, and environmental forces, as well as by inside policies, priorities, and available resources.

These facts suggest continuous monitoring and making appropriate changes in your strategic approach, if you are to optimize results. These changes include adjustments in your marketing mix – that is, the particular combination of marketing tools that you use at each stage (see Table 7.1).

	Marketing mix elements			
Life cycle stage	Product	Pricing	Distribution	Promotion
Introduction	Offer technically mature product, keep mix small	'Skim the cream' of price insensitive innovators through high introductory price	'Fill the pipeline' to the consumer; use indirect distribution through wholesalers	Create primary demand for product category, spend generously on extensive and intensive 'flight' advertising and the use of the Internet
Growth	Improve product; keep mix limited	Adjust price as needed to meet competition	Increase product presence and market penetration	Spend substantially on expansion of sales volume
Maturity	Distinguish your product from competition; expand your product offering to satisfy different market segments	Capitalize on price-sensitive demand by further reducing prices	Take over wholesaling function yourself by establishing distribution centres and having your own sales force call on retailers	Differentiate your product in the minds of prospective buyers; emphasize brand appeal
Saturation	Proliferate your mix further, diversify into new markets	Keep prices stable	Intensify your distribution to increase availability and exposure	Maintain the status quo; support your market position
Decline	Prune your mix radically	Carefully increase prices	Consolidate your distribution setup; establish minimum orders	Reduce advertising activity to reminder level

Table 7.1: Strategies throughout the product life cycle

Successful management of your product's life cycle requires careful planning and thorough understanding of its characteristics at the various points of the curve. Only then can you respond quickly and advantageously to new situations, leaving competitors in your wake. The following guidelines describe the strategies outlined in Table 7.1.

Introduction

In the introduction stage, it is the task of the pioneer to create primary demand – namely, demand for the new product category. Initially, keep the product mix small to provide a clear focus and keep costs under control. Also, confine the mix to just a few variations that reflect the underlying concept of the entire category. (Baby food, for example, was initially launched with a mix of only five products.)

As for your channel strategy, attempt to secure maximum availability of your product in the right outlets. It is essential to the success of your marketing effort that you obtain the support of middlemen and 'filling the pipeline' to the consumer. Choosing the right intermediaries is a difficult decision in itself, unless your channel is already set through your current relationships.

Also essential is the support given to your product in the form of advertising. Anything less than generous funding and an all-out advertising effort will reduce the product's chances for survival. Giving a new product lukewarm advertising support is generally tantamount to signing its death warrant.

With pricing, you have the option to set it fairly low – a strategy called penetration pricing – aimed at creating a mass market and discouraging competitive imitation through low unit profits and large investment requirements. Or you may consider a skimming strategy that starts out with a comparatively high price aimed at recovering your initial outlays for development and market introduction before competitive pressure erodes your temporary advantage.

Growth

In the growth stage, you will want to modify your basic product to take care of any problems discovered through initial consumer reactions. However, since the product category is selling so well, the product mix can remain small.

With regard to channels of distribution, your goals will include persuading current channel members to buy more and to sign up new channel members. This drive is greatly aided by booming demand, which strains the industry's supply capability and has distributors scurrying for merchandise. Your salespeople will continue to sell along the same lines as before, building upon the emerging success story of your innovation.

Your advertising emphasis is likely to shift somewhat from creating product awareness to expanding market volume. Prices soften as price-cutting competitors enter the market.

Maturity

Moving into the maturity phase can be traumatic, because the peaceful coexistence of competitors now turns into a fight for market share. At this time, it pays to redesign your product to make it more distinctive and easier to differentiate from competitive offerings. Since product technology is well developed, changes tend to be more cosmetic than functional.

The following three categories of strategies apply when a product reaches the troublesome mature stage of the product life cycle, where managers devote much of their trouble-shooting time:

1. Market modification

- Expand the number of users by converting non-users to your product, entering new market niches, and converting competitors' customers to your company.

- Increase customers' usage of your product by presenting ways to use the product more frequently, in greater quantities, and for more varied applications.

2. Product modification

- Utilize quality improvement to increase the product's functional performance, such as through durability, reliability, and speed.

- Add feature improvements that expand the product's versatility, safety, and convenience through size, materials, additives, or accessories.

- Implement style improvements using shape, packaging, colour and other aesthetic and functional modifications.

3. Marketing-mix modification

- Examine the wide range of non-product strategies connected with price, sales, advertising, service, and distribution.

Saturation

As your product enters the saturation stage of its life cycle, typically a no-holds-barred fight develops for market share. With market volume stabilizing, growth typically is achieved at the expense of competitors. In your product strategy, you will find yourself compelled to differentiate further by offering even more choice.

Also, it would pay to examine a strategy of diversification. Entering another field (if consistent with your strategic direction) could reduce your risk by decreasing your exposure to the fate of a particular product and could thus add stability, as well as potential revenue and profit, to your business.

Your supply chain strategy remains unaltered in the saturation phase. You should attempt to gain even more intensive distribution and, thereby, maximize availability and exposure. Toward this end, your salespeople will have to make a well planned, concerted effort to obtain more trade cooperation.

The primary function of advertising at this point is to maintain the status quo. Little new ground can be broken, so advertising of the reminder or reinforcement type is needed. Elasticity of demand reaches its highest point at this stage. This fact is of little strategic consequence, however, since most possibilities for cost reduction have been exhausted.

Decline

With consumer interest in the product waning in the decline phase, competitors drop out of the market in droves. If you are still in the market, you will trim your product offering to the bone, vigorously weeding out weak products and concentrating on a few unchanged items.

Similarly, you will attempt to reduce distribution cost by consolidating warehouses and sales offices, as well as establishing minimum orders to discourage small shipments. Your sales effort will tend to be low key, with an emphasis on retaining as much of your market as you can. Advertising support will diminish to the low-budget, infrequent-reminder type. Your prices will stay right about where they are.

Finally, studies have shown that the classic product life cycle pattern conforms reasonably well to reality. It remains a pragmatic and useful tool to monitor your product's life and to develop short – and long-term product strategies.

Product competition

Generating higher revenue

Overview: To gain a larger share of a total market, consider introducing additional products as competing lines or as private labels. The additional products provide a solid front against competitors. Overall, the strategy aims at generating higher revenue than does the use of only a single product.

The following case illustrates a significant application of product competition.

Symbian

This London-based company is a maker of a software operating system for mobile phones and handheld devices. Yet, this smallish company turns out to be a troublesome competitor to the mighty Microsoft Corporation. Overlaying the situation is an even greater dilemma for Microsoft: Symbian has created powerful joint-ventures with Nokia, Ericsson, Panasonic, Motorola, Siemens, and Samsung.

The core advantage, however, is that Symbian wields its powerful digital software for the next generation of products, such as wireless Web-surfing phones and souped-up mobile phones that will give callers access to the Internet. Symbian's aim is to disconnect the Net from desktops and phone lines. If Symbian prevails, these machines, from phones to palmtops, will run on Symbian O2 software – not on Microsoft's system for handheld machines. Symbian's goal is to become the industry and wireless standard.

The product competition has evolved as an all-out fight for market domination. Symbian, with its powerful partners, provide a solid customer base and a capability to produce and market its smart phones. Microsoft, not to be outdone, is busy signing up partners, from British Telecommunications PLC to Qualcomm Inc. of the U.S., to push handsets and other devices using its new Windows software.

Action strategy

What can you learn from the Symbian/Microsoft case? To develop competing products, make certain you apply a meaningful product differentiation strategy, and be certain you have a capability to reach a market with a substantial customer base.

Here are some useful guidelines for developing a competitive product:

- **Features and benefits**: Identify characteristics that complement your product's primary functions. Start with your basic product. Then add unique features and services; ideally, ones based on users' expectations.

- **Performance**: Relate to the level at which the product operates – including quality. Ideally, levels of performance should exceed those of competing products.

- **Acceptance**: Measure how close the product comes to established standards or specifications.

- **Endurance**: Tell of the product's expected operating life.

- **Dependability**: Measure the probability of the product breaking or malfunctioning within a specified period.

- **Appearance**: Cover numerous considerations ranging from image, function, look, or feel. Different from performance, appearance integrates the product with all its differentiating components, including packaging.

- **Design**: Unite the above differentiating components, as well. While design encompasses the product's appearance, endurance and dependability, there is particular emphasis placed on ease of use and appropriateness to the function for which it was designed.

Product mix

Creating a profit advantage

Overview: Evaluate the profit advantage of maintaining a single product concentrated in a specialized market. For growth and protection from competitors, however, consider a multiple-product strategy, which could include add-on products and services.

First, keep in mind the definition of a new product. A product is new when it is perceived as new by the prospect or customer. Therefore, new products can cover a range of innovations – from minor change to new to the world – if the changes are perceived as new. For example, modifying products for specialized applications, developing new forms of packaging, or devising a system for convenience of storage and retrieval, potentially qualify as a new product as long as it fits the above definition.

Further, by adding value through field technical assistance, computer-linked inventory systems, and technical/advisory telephone hookups, you can also give the impression of new.

The following checklist can help you get started on developing your product mix:

Step one: Review your company's strategic direction or overall product line objectives (review Chapter 5 on Strategic marketing planning). You thereby guard against venturing into line extensions that do not relate to your core business.

Step two: Define your market by sales and profit volume, customer usage, purchasing patterns, anticipated market share, and investment required.

Step three: Determine product development requirements, such as: using existing company technology, obtaining new technology, licensing finished products, or outsourcing an entire project.

Step four: Evaluate competitive offerings. Determine how to differentiate your new product to avoid a direct confrontation with look-alike products.

Step five: Determine the proposed product's position. Will you position it to defend a market niche or as an offensive move to secure additional market share? Will it be used as a probe to enter an emerging market or as a pre-emptive attack on competitors to discourage their entry?

Product design

Satisfying customer needs

Overview: The demands of the marketplace, the intensity of competition, and the flexibility of your company will dictate whether a standard, customized, or modified product is the optimum strategy.

Here is one system that works: Explore customers' needs and problems in two broad categories that would appeal to their self-interests: revenue-expansion and cost-reduction opportunities. This approach will score positive results for your customers. In due course, it should also help you provide applicable products and services.

To conduct the analysis, ask the following questions:

Revenue-expansion opportunities:

- What approaches would reduce customers' returns and complaints?
- What processes would speed-up production and delivery to benefit customers?
- How can you improve customers' market position and image?
- How would adding a name brand impact customers' revenue?
- What product or service benefits would enhance customers' operation?
- How can you create differentiation that gives customers a competitive advantage?
- How would improving re-ordering procedures impact revenues?

Cost-reduction opportunities:

- What procedures would cut customers' purchase costs?
- What processes would cut customers' production costs?
- What systems would cut customers' production downtime?
- What approaches would cut customers' delivery costs?
- What methods would cut customers' administrative over-heads?
- What strategies would maximize customers' working capital?

Several of those areas reach beyond the traditional role of marketing. Therefore, involve product developers and other non-marketing managers to interpret findings and translate them into product design solutions.

Finally, implementing the process is a sticky problem, particularly when it comes to involving non-marketing groups in actively thinking about such areas as customers' needs, market growth, and competitive advantage. There is no easy solution.

For starters, however, enlist the assistance of the senior executives in your group or company. Have them brief those non-marketing personnel on the benefits of paying attention to market-driven issues for the welfare of the company as well as their personal career growth – and survival. If that doesn't do the trick, you might recommend that an orientation seminar be used to help instill the appropriate attitudes.

New products/ services

Developing a competitive advantage

Overview: New products and services are the heart of any business that seeks to sustain growth and competitive advantage. The pace of new product introduction and obsolescence is so fast and rigorous that only one out of five innovations survive long enough in the marketplace to become a commercial success.

When the stakes are so high, it pays to improve your odds by gaining a better understanding of the new product process in all its ramifications. Sensitivity and adaptability are prerequisites for success in a dynamic marketplace where needs are constantly changing.

Defining a new product

Before defining what a new product is, you must first understand what a product is. It may seem perfectly obvious, since we deal with many products every day. A product is an object, device, or substance. But that definition hardly suffices in today's environment. It reduces the concept of a product to a combination of physical and chemical attributes in line with the old product-oriented concept of marketing.

This emphasis on tangible characteristics neglects the fact that intangibles – such as quality, colour, prestige, and back-up services – make a significant difference to a prospective buyer. A consumer perceives a product as a source of potential satisfaction, and may buy your offering to satisfy a particular want or desire rather than for its functional value. Charles Revson, the late founder of Revlon, in his now classic statement put it succinctly when he said: "In the factory, we make cosmetics; in the store, we sell hope."

As indicated earlier, a useful definition of a new product is where a customer perceives the offering as new. A product can be many things to many people. This definition places the emphasis on perception rather than on objective facts, and leaves much room for interpretation.

There is a reverse side to this emphasis on perception, though. If you have a product that has never before been offered for sale but is perceived by customers as more of the same, then you really do not have a 'new' product from a marketing point of view.

Category	Definition	Nature	Benefit
Modification	Altering a product feature	Same number of product lines and products	Combining the new with the familiar
Line extension	Adding more variety	Same number of product lines, higher number of products	Segmenting the market by offering more choice
Diversification	Entering a new business	New product line, higher number of products	Spreading risk and capitalizing on opportunities
Remerchandising	Marketing change to create a new impression	Same product, same markets	Generating excitement and stimulating sales
Market extension	Entering a new market	Same products, new market	Broadening the base

Table 7.2: Categories of new products

Categories of new products

New products come in many different forms. This diversity can be reduced to varying degrees of technological and marketing newness. In terms of increasing degrees of technological change, you may want to distinguish among modification, line extension, and diversification.

Table 7.2 presents the differences among these five categories of new products and points out the benefits of each.

Combined approach for new product categories

Rarely will the five categories of new products presented here be used separately. They lend themselves to combined applications for maximum impact. Moreover, you will probably want to avail yourself of a package approach to maintain steady growth in a rapidly changing environment.

Line extension, for example, is often used with remerchandising or market extension. Diversification is often combined with market extension. For increasing degrees of marketing newness, you can differentiate between re-merchandizing and market extension.

The use of one category does not preclude the application of other approaches at the same time, possibly within the same market. What remains essential, though, is that the prospective customer perceives a difference worthy of consideration.

Steps in the evolution of a new product

The genesis of an innovation occurs in a process called new product evolution. It takes place in a cyclical fashion with a four-stage format, as shown in Figure 7.2. These stages break down into a number of steps that detail the activities involved in bringing about a successful new product. The steps are presented in Table 7.3, together with their respective results.

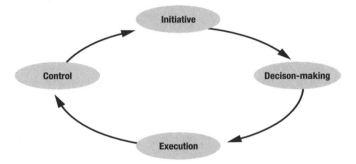

Figure 7.2: The cycle of new product evolution

PROCESS STEPS	RESULTS
Initiative	
1. Initiating forces	Get action under way
2. Perception and identification of problem or opportunity	Realize and pinpoint nature of challenge
Decision-making	
1. Definition of objectives and criteria	Set frame of reference
2. Start of comprehensive marketing research programme	Feed decision maker relevant information on continuous basis
3. Examination of market data	Provide factual input
4. Idea generation	Map out alternative courses of action
5. Screening	Weed out unpromising alternatives
6. Business analysis	Subject surviving proposals to in-depth scrutiny
7. Product development	Convert ideas into products
8. Market testing	Examine market acceptance
9. Finalize marketing programme	Prepare for rollout
10. Pilot production	Fill the pipeline
Execution	
1. Full-scale launch	Begin market introduction
2. Product life cycle	Analyze sales and profit changes
Control	
1. Continuous feedback of results	Compare planned and actual figures
2. Corrective action	Keep on course

Table 7.3: The process of new product evolution

Initiative

New products don't emerge from thin air. Rather, the initiating force is likely to reside with some astute manager within your organization who perceives a product concept and triggers the process that results in a profitable addition to your product mix.

Numerous external or internal factors (discussed in Chapter 1) can result in a new product initiative. They may reflect market, technological, competitive, or company developments. In any case, they constitute the motivating forces behind the evolutionary process.

Considering the rapid changes occurring in your environment, you should watch for early indications of potential threats and analyze them carefully for emerging new market opportunities. Forecasting, therefore, plays a crucial role in new product evolution by predicting alternative future environmental conditions or events, as well as the likelihood of their occurrence. Some companies even retain the services of an elite group of planners to speculate about such future scenarios.

Yet, there are more basic approaches for obtaining significant insights into market trends:

- Careful examination of consumer preferences and life styles, competitive new product activity, distribution patterns, and – most basic of all – sales and profit data. Increasingly, companies are creating collaborative relationships with customers to jointly develop new products, which goes as far as sharing technology data and operating systems.

- Technological developments can be just as stimulating. For example, new applications of lasers, glass fibres, and superconductors offer a host of opportunities for the imaginative manager. Lasers are actively employed in industry, surgery, and communications with remarkable results. Glass fibres are in the forefront of telecommunications and new customized computer chips have spawned an array of specialized new products at affordable prices to expose vast new markets.

- Increasingly, there is the immense potential of technology transfer. That is, applying to one field the technology developed in another. For example, Rockwell International Corporation, a major space contractor, used technology developed for the space programme in designing anti-skid devices for truck braking systems. Similarly, microwave ovens are an outgrowth of the space programme.

- Events within your firm may also be the source of a new product initiative. Such events may include suggestions by employees concerning improvement of existing products or development of entirely different ones.

- Purchasing problems involving limited availability of key materials or price increases for energy may trigger a rethinking process for new products.

- Sales trends can and should bring about a re-evaluation of your current and future situation, often resulting in new product programmes.

While there are numerous environmental clues, your firm will not profit from them unless someone in your organization is sensitive enough to respond selectively to them. Typically, this person will be the product manager of a given product line. More than any other, this person is called upon to scan facts and developments and identify those that represent legitimate problems that, in turn, can be converted to a product opportunity.

New product decision-making

The sequence of new product evolution begins with goal setting and ends with initial production. In between is a series of crucial steps that will determine the success of your venture in the marketplace. Close attention to each of the following steps is essential.

Defining objectives and criteria

Typically, new product objectives involve growth targets with outcomes measured by increases in sales volume and market share. However, they often remain non-operational, since they are interpreted by criteria. The latter are instruments of measurement that translate objectives into operational form.

Research and examination of market data

While it is the role of objectives and criteria to guide the evolutionary effort and keep it on course, it is the job of ongoing marketing research to supply the decision-maker with the relevant facts. The task, then, is to hook up with the consumer and establish communication links that keep the evolutionary process going efficiently and on course.

The body of data generated in the first round of this marketing research programme is then screened for usable information capable of triggering dynamic thinking. The following process, attributed to management consultants, Booze Allen Hamilton Inc., is a reliable product development system you can emulate:

Phase 1: Idea generation. Once a database has been established, idea generation can begin. At this early stage, many ideas are necessary for an ultimate yield of one successfully commercialized product. Booze Allen Hamilton put this ratio at 58:1. Scrutiny becomes more and more rigorous as a product idea advances from its genesis. All the more reason to generate as many ideas as possible at the outset. Also at this point, as you search for alternative courses of action don't concern yourself with such issues as feasibility or profitability.

Tap a wide range of sources for product ideas: internal sources such as top management, research and development people, marketing personnel, and other employees. Also use a variety of external sources such as consumers, middlemen, competitors, scientists, inventors, research labs, and suppliers. The techniques employed in activating these sources range from brainstorming to various surveying methods.

Phase 2: Idea screening. Assuming you have generated a wealth of new product ideas, they should be subjected to a screening procedure. This step aims to weed out unpromising ideas before they become costly in time, effort, and money. Thus, the goal is to eliminate from further consideration as many ideas as possible. Two thirds to three-quarters of the original ideas vanish at this point.

The focus now is to examine questions of feasibility and profitability. Neither of the two, after all, can exist without the other: Feasible products that are not profitable are simply giveaways; profitable products that are not feasible are fiction.

The issue of feasibility may be general (whether appropriate technology exists) or specific (whether your R&D and production departments can handle the job). Profitability, on the other hand, involves projections of anticipated price levels and unit costs to decide whether there is enough money in a deal to warrant your attention.

Phase 3: Business analysis. The few ideas that pass the screening test enter the business analysis stage. They now receive in-depth scrutiny. The purpose of this step is to advise top management whether it should authorize certain proposals as development projects. Therefore, a careful impact statement has to be developed for each concept, with thorough projections of what would happen if it were adopted and converted into a real product.

Management must know the consequences to your firm in terms of required technological know-how, production and salesforce utilization, image, morale, and – most of all – finances. A concept test is likely to help you in assessing consumer reaction and preference at this point.

Your financial analysis also has to be much more thorough at this stage than during screening, relying on tools such as breakeven analysis (to determine the sales volume needed to cover costs) and differential accounting (to compute the return on investment).

Phase 4: Product development and market testing. Once a particular idea has tested well and has received top management's blessing, it is assigned to personnel for conversion into a tangible product. Here, technical and production people go to work with clear-cut specifications. They will develop rough drafts that will be tested and refined, until the product is completely debugged and ready for full-scale production.

Of course, before you begin full-scale production, test a sample quantity among users, asking them to try your product at your expense and then suggest changes to improve its performance or enhance its appeal. This procedure – product testing – is intended to help you modify and finalize the product design.

The most popular approach to product testing involves matching your product against that of a major competitor to find out which product your audience prefers and why. The results cannot be taken as conclusive evidence, however, since you select the participants and give them the products.

Therefore, the true indication of your innovation's full market potential is explored only by means of test marketing. This activity involves introducing your product in a number of test cities (or market segments) to see how well it will sell under real market conditions.

It is important that these test markets be representative of your overall market and that you run the test long enough to establish repurchase patterns. After all, it is relatively easy to sell somebody something for the first time. The real test is whether the customer buys it again. This measurement cannot be made through sales audits alone, but requires customer interviews as well.

Interviews are costly, thus making test marketing expensive and threatening. Threatening means that your competitor's intelligence system may detect your findings and attempt to blunt your efforts if you decide on a roll-out with full market coverage.

Phase 5: Final marketing programme and pilot production. Completion of market testing enables you to put the finishing touches on your marketing programme by adjusting certain elements of your marketing mix for maximum effectiveness.

This adjustment permits you to get ready for a full-scale roll-out. Of course, you first have to go through pilot production; that is, produce enough merchandise to satisfy initial demand. This step completes the decision-making phase of new product evolution.

Phase 6: Execution and control. Once you complete the internal development and external testing of your new product, you are ready to launch its full-scale market introduction. Your revised introductory programme should now set in motion the start of your product's life cycle, which goes from introduction through growth and maturity, and then to saturation and decline.

Even the best planning cannot foresee all possible events. Therefore continuous feedback to monitor the effectiveness of your product strategy is necessary. This feedback enables periodic comparisons between planned and actual figures. In turn, you can take corrective action to keep your programme on course. Ultimately this action may result in initiating another evolutionary process that could displace the current product.

Finally, there is another perspective to consider: the commitment to service as part of your new product strategy, particularly in price-sensitive markets.

Commitment to service

Overlaying the entire new product process is an attitude and commitment to render superior service as part of your strategy. Some well-known companies have gained notoriety with their obsession for delivering extraordinary service, among them: McDonalds, Marriott, and Disney.

What has emerged from these companies dedicated to a service strategy are the following guidelines for executing a service strategy as part of your new product development effort:

- **Customer obsession**: All levels of employees (those with and without direct customer contact) must understand what makes your customers tick. They should sense what tangible and intangible services would satisfy customers and result in long-term loyalty.

- **Commitment to high standards**: To behave as a service-oriented company, you must set high standards and be able to measure results. For instance, a division of 3M cut its complaint handling time from 49 days to 5 days. Managers then monitored ongoing performance not only within their own operation but used the new standard as a benchmark of performance against competitors.

- **Procedures to monitor service performance**: Begin with some easy-to-use methods to monitor your service performance, such as: formal surveys among customers, informal visits to customers by marketing and technical personnel, and watching the mail for unresolved problems or clues that may lead to new services.

The key, however, is to collect feedback from all sources on a regular schedule. Then, assemble the data into a functional report that measures actual performance with customers' expectations. In the same report, compare the level of service you provide with that of your primary competitors. Finally, share the report with those who can take positive action to improve service performance.

- **Responsiveness to customers' needs**: Speed, accuracy, and effective communications form the underpinnings for first-class service performance. All that monitoring systems can accomplish is to red flag what remedial action is needed. Ultimately, the decisive difference in sustaining customer satisfaction and maintaining a competitive advantage is how your firm resolves product problems, handles quality issues, meets delivery dates, and delivers the myriad of other meaningful services.

Product audit

Maintaining product-line control

Overview: Knowing when to pull a product from the line is as important as knowing when to introduce a new one. Appropriate to the task is to consider such internal requirements as profitability, available resources, and new growth opportunities. Also examine external factors of salesforce coverage, dealer commitment, and customers' needs to determine if a comprehensive line is required.

Overall, however, efficient use of the product audit is one of the reliable procedures for sustaining product-line profitability. The following examples illustrate the application.

Examples

Kraft, Colgate-Palmolive, Toyota, Nabisco, Procter & Gamble, and other market-driven organizations are pursuing a dominant trend. All are focusing on fresh approaches to improve the profitability of their product lines.

While many organizations have pursued product profitability over the past decade through downsizing, re-engineering, and similar high-profile approaches, what is significant this time are the techniques those companies use to directly impact their marketing efforts.

Increasingly, they deal with product profitability by looking to such marketing-related activities as:

- standardizing product packages

- reducing trade promotions

- pulling back on couponing

- trimming product lines

- decreasing the number of new product launches.

For example, Nabisco cut its product line by 15% and reduced new product launches by 20%. Kraft initiated moves for the cereal industry to stabilize list prices. Clorox simplified its trade promotions and reduced the number of items it sells. General Motors reduced the number of car models from 53 to 44.

Procter & Gamble, in particular, illustrates the significant potential for profitability. It has reduced its product line-up by one third since 1990. In hair products alone, it cut the number of sizes, packages, and formulas in half, while watching with satisfaction as market share in hair-care jumped nearly five points to 36.5%. In the shampoo line, P&G standardized product formulas and packages to just two basic packages, saving an extraordinary $25 million in one year.

What evidence supports this move toward a simplification of the marketing effort? First, an analysis of consumer goods sales by one consulting firm revealed the enlightening statistic that almost 25% of the products in a typical supermarket sell less than one unit a month. What's more, just 7.6% of all personal care and household products account for 84.5% of sales.

These statistics validate the often-quoted 80/20 rule, whereby 80% of sales (and anything else) come from 20% of customers. Nevertheless, how does all this affect the governing rule of market segmentation, whereby managers are counselled to target emerging, neglected, and poorly served markets and then cater to each segment with customized products and services?

Does the trend now reverse the use of a segmentation strategy? Not at all. Segmentation, targeting, and concentrating on customers are practical, workable, and successful strategies. Rather, the faults lie, in part, with the lack of attention given to sorting out and interpreting the vast amount of data generated by today's sophisticated electronic measurement devices.

When accurate market information pinpoints those market segments that would respond favourably to your marketing efforts, then implementing your marketing strategies should improve product-line profitability.

Action strategy

To implement several of the above guidelines, you can use an easy-to-install procedure: a product audit. Just as regular physical examinations are essential to maintain the body's good health, like-wise, products require regular examination to determine whether they are healthy, need repromotion, or should be allowed to phase out.

Begin your product audit by setting up a product audit committee (see details below). The product audit can assist you in accomplishing the following:

- Determine your product's long-term market potential.

- Assess the advantages and disadvantages of adding value to the product.

- Alter your product's market position compared to that of a competitor's comparable product.

- Evaluate the chances of your product being displaced by another product or technology.

- Calculate the product's contribution to your company's financial goals.

- Judge if the product-line is filled out sufficiently to prevent your customers from shopping elsewhere.

In addition to the above criteria, consider such issues as availability of money and human resources, assessment of new product and market growth opportunities, and even the effective use of your executives' time. Also, add such factors as your firm's willingness to sustain salesforce coverage, dealer commitment, and ongoing eagerness to respond to changing customers' needs.

Finally, phasing out weak products or exiting a market requires careful consideration of your company's obligations. For instance, there may be significant costs related to labour agreements, maintaining capabilities for spare parts, contractual relationships with dealers and distributors, financial institutions, etc. In sum, the product audit provides a practical approach to your decision-making process.

Establishing a product audit program

The first step in establishing a regular product evaluation programme is to create a product audit committee. This core group, comprised of the top people in the marketing, finance, engineering, and purchasing departments, should control decision-making about the design of the company's product mix. Depending upon the dimensions of the product mix and the significance of the products or developments involved, the product audit committee should meet monthly, and every product should have at least an annual review.

How does such a committee operate? To do justice to each product and to have an objective basis for product comparisons, a common rating form should be used. For products that appear dubious, and thus demand careful evaluation, you can use a product audit form similar to the one illustrated in Figure 7.3.

Using a simple 1 to 5 scoring system, you can assign values for each of eight criteria. Some of these values will necessarily be subjective in nature, with 1 representing strong grounds for eliminating the product and a score of 5 suggesting retention.

In each case, the score reflects the majority opinion or consensus of the committee. For greater accuracy, each criterion can be given a degree of importance or weight. These weights are then multiplied by the appropriate score and totalled to form the specific product retention index.

Product/service criteria	High				Low
	1	2	3	4	5
1. What is the market potential for the product? Assign a score based on dollar value, unit volume, or other quantitative measures.					
2. What competitive advantage might be gained by adding value, modifying the product, or creating other differentiation features and benefits?					
3. What would be gained by positioning the product differently to customers and against competing products?					
4. How many resources (materials, equipment, people, and dollars) would be available by eliminating the product?					
5. How good are the opportunities to redeploy resources to a new product, service, or business?					
6. Based on financial calculation of ROI, profits, and any other key financial criteria, how much is the product contributing beyond its direct costs?					
7. What value does the product have in supporting the sale of other company products?					
8. Is the product useful in defending a point of entry against competitors?					

Figure 7.3: Product rating form

In contrast to accounting audits, product audits are conducted strictly for internal purposes. They should be part of a regular programme, practised consistently and continuously. Products that are no longer earning their keep should be eliminated without delay or sentimentality, provided that such a move has no negative repercussions for the remaining members of the product family. Such pruning frees valuable resources that provide the basis for growth through new products.

Best practices

Anticipate a competitor's move into your marketplace by developing a competing product or service. Recognize early the potentials of new technology, particularly in areas where competitors may choose not to invest. Also use life cycle extensions as the mainstay of your strategy. Whenever possible, pre-empt competitors' strategies and blunt their efforts to take market share from you.

To identify strategies and initiate action:

1. List product strategies that represent your best opportunities.

2. Include value-added services and product features that create differentiation.

3. Initiate market tests (or immediate full-market roll-out) and set in motion market penetration plans.

4. Monitor sales performance, obtain ongoing customer feedback, and relate them to your product objectives and the strategies employed.

5. Based on performance, take needed corrective action and set plans for future courses of action.

8

How to manage your communications strategy

Chapter objectives

Developing a successful advertising campaign

Determining your advertising budget

Guidelines for successful sales promotion

How to use sales promotion to stimulate sales

Marketing over the Internet

Best practices

Chapter objectives

After reading this chapter, you should be able to:

- Develop a successful advertising campaign.
- Use sales promotion to stimulate sales.
- Convert promotion strategies into action.
- Identify ways to utilize the internet.

A marketing database is the bedrock of relationship marketing. Armed with a mixture of various insights on habits and buying behaviour, you will be in a superior position to find, keep, and communicate accurately with your customers and prospects.

Even if you don't currently have such a database, such a system of acquiring data currently exists through the Internet. With the growth of technology, the entire process of information gathering – which is part of the broader system of data warehousing and data mining – will continue to grow with explosive intensity to reveal exacting information about customers and prospects.

Software can monitor customer orders and tastes. Generally known as behavioural targeting, it tracks buying trends across hundreds of web sites and phone calls from customers, observes how many times a web visitor checks out an advertisement or a product (and what they avoid), and traces patterns of in-store behaviour.

Specifically, available software and database programs can fill critical knowledge gaps about customers, products, and services. The result: You, or those responsible for developing an advertising campaign, can create more responsive advertising to:

- Add precision to targeting viable markets.
- Promote customized products and services for different market segments, as well as by an individual's buying patterns.
- Improve customer retention.
- Communicate trends in buying behaviour to product and service developers – or suppliers.

The following examples illustrate the practical applications of correctly profiling a customer to maximize communication effectiveness:

- **NextCard Inc.**, an issuer of credit cards, advertises its service on a financial website. A prospect clicks the advertisement promising quick approval and reviews a choice of terms based on his/her specific needs. After filling out a short on-line form that provides profile information and credit history, in seconds the prospect's approval appears on the screen. Behind the scenes, NextCard's computers dialled three major credit bureaus to check the prospect's financial background. With dazzling speed from 30,000 potential combinations of credit card terms in its product portfolio, three offers were submitted tailored to the prospect's profile.

The result: NextCard obtained exacting profile information, created a tailored offering, and won a new customer in microseconds – instead of the usual three to six weeks to issue a card and transfer balances.

- **Matsushita Electric Industrial**, the consumer-electronics giant, conducted an on-line survey of subscribers to its Internet access service about the gifts they had bought or planned to buy. Matsushita then shared those results with its customers, such as department stores, dealers, and mail-order businesses, which parlayed the feedback into tailored advertising messages that resulted in a surge of new sales.

- **Abbey National**, a medium-size bank, uses precise customer profile data to sell mortgages, unsecured loans, and other financial products over the phone to qualified prospects. Closures on sales calls improved dramatically by sales people armed with the prospects' profiles. Through its network of 21 sites in Britain – plus new operations in Spain, France, and Italy – Abbey National is recording striking results as it tries to grab business from larger rivals such as Barclays Bank or Lloyds with speed and above all, reliable data about their prospects.

Core issues

These case examples reveal several core issues: If you assemble valid customer profiles that reveal detailed information of needs or problems, you are in an optimum position to develop benefit-oriented advertising that attracts prospects. In turn, you position yourself in the best-selling situation to customize a product or service offering. Doing so also maximizes your chances of making a sale based on solid knowledge of customer behaviour, as opposed to merely presenting a generic hit-or-miss product to prospects based on borderline, undocumented information.

Consequently, when developing your promotion effort keep these two fundamental issues in the forefront of your thinking:

1. Know the behaviour of your market and develop accurate individual profiles of customers and prospects from a variety of

sources (Internet technology and data mining software provide the most accurate and reliable data sources).

2. Determine buyer patterns, including ability to buy, a purchasing timeframe, and usage patterns. Then you can develop an effective communications strategy that combines advertising, sales promotion, and increasingly the heavy use of the Internet into a totally integrated force. Within that framework, let's begin with advertising strategies and how to develop a successful campaign.

Developing a successful advertising campaign

Advertising is any paid form of non-personal presentation and promotion of ideas, goods, or services by an identified sponsor. Moreover, advertising is but one component of promotion; and promotion is just one component of the marketing mix. Thus, advertising – as with all the other parts of the marketing mix (product, pricing, and distribution) – is never created in isolation.

Responsibilities of advertising

Initially, you should know the job you want advertising to accomplish. There are broad responsibilities, such as:

1. Informing your target audience about the availability and features of your product or service.

2. Persuading your prospect to buy your product.

3. Reducing the cost of selling.

Then, there are specific responsibilities associated with advertising:

- Support personal selling.

- Achieve a specific number of exposures to your target audience.

- Address persons who are inaccessible to salespeople.

- Create a specified level of product awareness, measurable through recall or recognition tests.

- Improve dealer relations.

- Increase product usage.

- Improve customer attitudes toward your company or product.

- Introduce a new product or service and generate demand for it.

- Build familiarity and easy recognition of your company, brand, package, or trademark.

- Counteract false impressions about the company or product.

The list is endless and as varied as companies and situations. It illustrates some of the possibilities and pinpoints the need for precision to derive maximum benefits from objectives. Because objectives imply accountability for results, they often lead to an evaluation of individual or agency performance.

Once you clearly define what you want to accomplish, then you can choose media and copy themes to match those objectives. As a result, your advertising becomes defined, realistic, measurable, and result-oriented.

Guidelines for a successful advertising campaign

Now that you have selected advertising objectives, here are some key points you need to know to develop a successful advertising campaign – or critique one that is submitted to you for approval.

Table 8.1 details the steps involved in developing an advertising campaign. As already indicated, it shows clearly that continuous marketing research is the foundation of a sound campaign.

Campaign step	Advertising activities	Research activities
1. Market analysis	*Pre-campaign phase*	Study competitive products, positioning, media, distribution, and usage patterns
2. Product research		Identify perceived product characteristics and benefits
3. Customer research		Conduct demographic and psychographic (life style) studies of prospective customers; investigate media, purchasing, and consumption patterns
4. Set advertising objectives	*Strategic decisions* Determine target markets and market targets (user profile, exposure goals)	
5. Decide on level of appropriation	Determine total advertising spending necessary to support objectives	Investigate competitive spending levels and media costs necessary to reach objectives
6. Formulate advertising strategy	Develop creative approach and prepare 'shopping list' of appropriate media	Examine audience profiles, reach, frequency, and costs of alternative media
7. Integrate advertising strategy with overall marketing strategy	Make sure that advertising supports and is supported by other elements of the marketing mix	
8. Develop detailed advertising budget	*Tactical execution* Break down overall allocation to spending on media categories and individual media	
9. Choose message content and mode of presentation	Develop alternative creative concepts, copy, and layout	Conduct concept and copy tests
10. Analyze legal ramifications	Have selected copy reviewed by legal staff or counsel	
11. Establish media plan	Determine media mix and schedule	Conduct media research, primarily from secondary sources
12. Review agency presentation	See entire planned campaign in perspective for approval	

13. Production and traffic	**Campaign implementation** Finalize and reproduce advertisement(s), buy media time and space, and deliver ads	
14. Insertion of advertisements	Actually run ads in chosen media	Check whether ads appeared as agreed and directed
15. Impact control	**Campaign follow-through**	Get feedback on consumer and competitive reaction
16. Review and revision	Adjust advertising execution or spending levels to conditions	Check whether changes made yielded desired results

Table 8.1: Developing an advertising campaign

Situation analysis in the pre-campaign phase

Sound planning techniques call for a careful assessment of overall market conditions before formulating an advertising campaign. Follow these three steps:

1. Conduct a market analysis that surveys the competitive field during the pre-campaign phase. For instance, this analysis should examine the range of competitive offerings and related market trends, their positioning and media choices, and their distribution and usage patterns. You will want to find out who competitors' customers are and when, where, and for what purpose they make purchases. This background information will provide the necessary perspective for choosing appropriate promotion strategies.

2. In subsequent product research, focus more intensively on your own product. Its principal purpose is to find out from actual or potential users of the product which features they consider desirable and what benefits they associate with its use. Such information will help you make the right positioning decision and formulate effective appeals. In this context, study the usage patterns in depth.

3. Concentrate on the customer. Here you attempt to develop demographic and psychographic profiles of actual or prospective buyers. For instance, recognize who are the frequent and infrequent users of your product, how old they are, where they live, how much money they have at their disposal, their educational backgrounds, their occupations, their marital status and family size, and the cultural group they belong to.

You will also want to know how they think and act, to the extent that you have access to psychologists, sociologists, and anthropologists who can provide you with usable profiles. Ongoing research provides answers regarding their attitudes, interests, and opinions, which should help determine what motivates them.

You must then analyze their media habits. Knowing who your customers are and how they behave is of little value unless you know what they watch, listen to, and read. You need to know how to reach them. It is also helpful to find out where they purchase, how much, and how often, and who does the purchasing. Additional insights can be gained from a look at consumption patterns. At that point, you can determine who ultimately consumes your product, when, how much, how often, and under what circumstances.

Only after all of this preliminary information has been gathered, interpreted, and internalized should the advertising planning be initiated.

Making strategic decisions

Once the relevant data have been assembled and examined, you are ready to make a number of strategic decisions that will guide the detailed work that follows. As in all planning activities, the first major decision is to set advertising objectives from the list presented earlier.

Determining your advertising budget

Having decided on your objectives, you must now decide how best to get there. Marketing executives can choose from a number of alternative approaches for setting the level of total advertising spending.

- **Affordable method**: Ignores your objectives and is simply an allocation of how much you think you can afford to spend. This viewpoint makes your level of appropriation subject to guessing and may result in grossly over or under-estimating the amount in relation to your needs.

- **Percentage of sales approach**: Probably the most widely used because of its simplicity. That is, it ties your advertising allowance to a specified percentage of current or expected future sales. This procedure, with its built-in fluctuations, not only discourages long-term advertising planning but also neglects current business needs and opportunities.

- **Competitive parity method**: Proposes that your company matches competitive spending levels. This simplistic outlook is no more sophisticated or justifiable than the two preceding approaches.

- **Objective and task method**: Produces the most meaningful results. You proceed in three steps:
    1. Define your advertising objectives as specifically as possible.
    2. Identify the tasks that must be performed to achieve your objectives.
    3. Estimate the costs of performing these tasks. The sum total of these costs represents your level of appropriation. While this approach does not examine or justify the objectives themselves, nevertheless it reflects a reliable assessment of your perceived needs and opportunities, which you can translate into a workable budget.

Making your advertising investment more productive

Advertising is a key element in a total communications strategy. But remember, no matter how good your agency or advertising department is, you bear the ultimate responsibility for results. Therefore, it pays to be sceptical, knowledgeable, and to avoid being intimidated by the creators of your advertising.

Also remember that advertising can run into a significant sum of money in terms of total outlay, so you will want to make sure that your ads are working hard for you.

Finally, and most important, work more intelligently and effectively with your advertising people. For instance, offer more precise guidance by assembling reliable market data and customer buying information to provide as useful a customer profile as possible (or require your advertising people or market researchers to handle it for you). Then follow these fundamental guidelines:

1. **Be aware of your product's positioning in the marketplace**. You may choose to offer it as an alternative to an exciting way of doing things or to the competing product in the field. Also, emphasize a major customer differentiating benefit that is unique, meaningful, and competitive – one that you can convincingly deliver to the market.

2. **Maintain a personality for your brand**. Use your advertising to make a positive contribution to the brand image. If you want

177

your ads to command attention and produce results, try for a uniqueness that makes them stand out from the flood of competing messages. It is helpful to use a symbol, logo, or other repetitive element that will be remembered by customers.

3. **Don't bore your audience and don't be impersonal**. In particular, there are sufficient tools available, especially through Internet advertising, to personalize your advertising by gender, geographic location, and buying patterns. Also innovate, don't imitate. Start trends instead of following them. (Just be sure you know what trends to follow.) The risks are high, but so are the potential rewards.

4. **Be factual where you have substantive back-up information for your claims**. One powerful way to present factual material is to use a problem-solving approach. Choose a problem that your customer can relate to and show how your product can solve it.

5. **Formulate effective headlines**. Use simple, understandable language. Department store advertising research has shown that headlines of ten or more words sell more merchandise than shorter ones do. Understandably, recall is best for headlines of eight to ten words.

6. **Visually reinforce your advertising with illustrations, particularly of demonstrations**. Also, pictures with story and situational appeals awaken the curiosity of the readers and involve them in the text. Photographs almost invariably pull better than drawings. They attract more readers, generate more appetite appeal, are more believable, result in higher recall and coupon redemption, and produce more sales.

7. **Use captions, the capsule explanations beneath pictures, to sell**. Include your product's brand name and the major benefit you promise.

8. **Generate an informative atmosphere**. Giving your ads an editorial appearance may prove more productive than using elaborate, 'creative' layouts.

9. **Be aware that readership falls off rapidly in ad copy of up to 50 words, but shrinks only insignificantly in copy of 50 to 500 words**. Although relatively few people read long copy, those people generally represent genuine prospects. Studies show that those industrial ads with more than 350 words are read more thoroughly than shorter ones. (However,

avoid long-winded TV commercials. Let the action speak for itself.)

10. **Don't replace your advertisements before they have had a chance to develop their full potential**. The most basic learning theories stress the importance of repetition in affecting behaviour. Repeat your winners until their effects start to wear off.

Use the above list as guidelines that are rooted in decades of recorded advertising experience. However, just as styles change so too do the so-called trustworthy advertising principles. Therefore, consider these guidelines as a screening process to initially assess the creative output and produce a constructive dialogue with those who are creating the advertising.

Guidelines for successful sales promotion

Your overall objectives in utilizing sales promotion are to encourage more product usage, induce dealer involvement, and stimulate greater salesforce efforts.

The following examples illustrate varied applications of sales promotion to rebuild sales, maintain contact with customers, and penetrate additional markets.

- Oracle Corporation, the software maker, sells to companies in Europe, the Middle East, and Africa from its Dublin facility, with promotional incentives to encourage more product usage with its lower-priced software packages. That frees up Oracle's field salesforce to focus on more complex sales of higher value.

- General Motors Corporation's Opel unit in Antwerp maintains ongoing contact with dealers and customers alike to deal with problems that car owners encounter with their vehicles. It also supports dealers with software that links them to GM distribution centres.

- Coca-Cola, in its Hungry operation, shifted from 90% advertising to a 50-50 split between advertising and sales promotion. The strategy is geared to appeal to the local needs and attitudes of specific market segments (mostly younger groups), rather than the broad-based themes usually used in its general advertising. 'You've got to capture consumers with an experience,' declares a Coke executive. Sales promotion gives Coke more options to localize its marketing efforts.

Applications

What can you learn from these examples? While it may be difficult to match the diverse applications of sales promotion, you should internalize the enormous potential and variety of sales promotion uses and learn how to make them part of a total marketing strategy.

First, consider some characteristics of effective sales promotion. Sales promotion is an incentive to buy, whereas advertising offers a reason to buy. Also, while sales promotion is part of an overall marketing programme, it involves a variety of company functions to make it work effectively.

Second, sales promotion permits tremendous flexibility, creativity, and application. Look at the following applications:

- **Consumer promotions**: Consists of samples, coupons, cash refunds, premiums, free trials, warranties, and demonstrations.

- **Trade promotions**: Includes buying allowances, free goods, cooperative advertising, display allowances, push money, video conferencing, and dealer sales contests.

- **Sales force promotions**: Employs bonuses, contests, and sales rallies.

As indicated with advertising (and all other components of the marketing mix), sales promotion is not a stand-alone activity. Instead, make it a component of the tactical portion of your strategic marketing plan. Further, establish your sales promotion objectives to support the broader vision, or strategic direction.

Objectives include:

1. Entering new market segments

2. Gaining entry into new channels of distribution

3. Encouraging purchase of larger size units

4. Building trial usage among non-users

5. Attracting switchers away from competitors

6. Building brand loyalty

7. Stimulating off-season sales

8. Winning back customers.

How to use sales promotion to stimulate sales

Sales promotion can be an effective component of almost any promotion mix, ranging from consumer goods to industrial goods and even services, dynamically supplementing and complementing the more sophisticated advertising and personal selling efforts.

What is sales promotion? It consists of all those promotional efforts of a firm that cannot be grouped under the heading of advertising, personal selling, publicity, or packaging. More precisely, *sales promotion consists of activities or objects initiated by a seller that encourage salespeople, resellers, and ultimately buyers to take a prescribed action by temporarily offering extra value for money – or by providing some special incentive related to a product or service.*

While somewhat lengthy, this definition points out a number of essential features:

- Sales promotion includes both *activities* – such as demonstrations and contests, and *objects* – such as coupons, premiums, and samples.

- It may be directed at one or any combination of *three distinct audiences*: a company's own salesforce; middlemen of all types and levels, such as dealers, wholesalers and retailers; and consumers or commercial buyers.

- In contrast with the continuous, long-term nature of the other elements of the promotion mix, sales promotion campaigns are temporary measures that should be used with discretion.

Unless used wisely, sales promotion can easily become self-defeating and counter-productive. While there are no hard and fast rules, a brand, for example, that is 'on deal' one-third of the time or more is likely to suffer image problems. In fact, if yours is a leading brand in a mature market, you should use sales promotion sparingly because it is improbable that you will gain any lasting advantage from a more generous application.

It is important to remember that sales promotion is costly and should thus be judged from a cost/benefit point of view. So, don't over use it – even if the temptation is great to yield to internal pressures or external competitive challenges.

Nevertheless, sales promotion has experienced a phenomenal growth that can be expected to increase rapidly. Both internal and external factors have contributed to this impressive record.

181

Internal factors

First, senior management has come to view sales promotion as an acceptable and effective stimulant to sales, abandoning the long-held premise that hawking one's wares cheapens the brand.

Second, a more professional approach to sales promotion seeks to employ better-qualified individuals and upgrade their status within the organization.

Third, product managers now tend to be more receptive to the 'quick fix' aspects of sales promotion that helps them achieve fast and impressive results.

External factors

Some important reasons for increasing the use of sales promotion include:

- The number of products in the commercial and consumer marketplace has expanded, leading to intensified competition and the need to create more 'noise' at the point of purchase.

- There is a need to respond to competitive increases in promotion spending, although there is a clear danger of escalating into a 'war' in which all sides lose.

- In a recessionary economy, manufacturers are more willing to use rebates to shrink inventories and improve liquidity, just as consumers tend to be more responsive to sales stimulation measures.

- The growing power of, and pressure from, the trade produces more promotional allowances and support from suppliers.

Beginning a sales promotion campaign

To plan an effective approach to sales promotion, you will find it profitable to follow a series of logical steps to maximize impact and efficiency. This is achieved only if a sales promotion campaign is undertaken not in isolation, but as a part of a long-term plan, carefully integrated with the other elements of your firm's promotion mix and, ultimately, with the entire marketing mix.

The following steps are involved in developing a sales promotion campaign:

1. Establish your objective

2. Select appropriate promotional techniques

3. Develop your sales promotion program

4. Pretest your sales promotion program

5. Implement and evaluate your campaign.

Establish sales promotion objectives

While the main purpose of sales promotion is to increase the sales volume of a product or to stimulate traffic to a retail outlet or an Internet website, more specific objectives can be identified, depending upon the type of audience and the nature of the task involved. Sales promotion efforts, for instance, directed at your company's own salesforce aim to generate enthusiasm and zeal. It is important, then, that you offer your salespeople special incentives to excite them, along with follow-up support.

A second targeted group is your company's dealers or distributors, without whose active cooperation your entire marketing effort and, more specifically, a sales promotion campaign would falter. Lastly, while the support and loyalty of your salesforce and dealer/distributor network are certainly crucial, a sales promotion campaign would hardly be complete if it failed to stimulate buyer action.

Consider these objectives:

- Identify and attract new buyers.

- Encourage more frequent and varied usage of current products.

- Motivate trial and purchase of new products.

- Educate users and non-users about improved product features.

- Suggest purchases of multiple and/or larger units of your product.

- Win over buyers of competitive products.

- Reinforce brand loyalty and purchase continuity.

- Create customer enthusiasm and excitement leading to word-of-mouth recommendations and referrals.

- Diminish fluctuations by encouraging off-season usage.

- Counter competitive raiding.

- Generate more traffic at your dealers' outlets.

Although sales promotion campaigns represent short-term stimulation, they are most effective when used in a long-term framework. Further, sales promotion objectives should not be developed in a vacuum, rather, tie them in to your overall marketing strategies. In addition, make your sales promotion objectives audience-specific and use quantitative measures to facilitate later evaluation.

Select appropriate promotional techniques

Once you have decided which market segments you want to address, you can select specific techniques for motivating the dealer, introducing new products, and promoting existing products.

- **Motivating the dealer**: With dealers (or any intermediary in the industrial, consumer, and service sector), the most powerful language to speak is still money; that is, profit. Among many available techniques, sales promotion for motivating dealers can include buying allowances, cooperative advertising, dealer listings, sales contests, specialty advertising, and featured exhibits at trade shows.

- **Introducing new products**: Another meaningful way to break down the variety of approaches is to group them according to their major application area. Sales promotion techniques particularly well suited to the introduction of new products include free samples or trial offers, coupons, and money refunds.

- **Promoting existing products**: You may want to use one or more different tools when attempting to promote established brands, such as: premiums, price packs, contests and sweepstakes, trading stamps, and demonstrations. These tools aim to attract competitors' customers and build market share, introduce new versions of established brands, and reward buyer loyalty.

Table 8.2 will aid your selection process by presenting the advantages and disadvantages of these sales promotion techniques.

Techniques	Advantages	Disadvantages
Free samples	Induce trial Attract new customers Speed-up adoption	Expensive Lacks precision Cumbersome
Free trial	Overcomes market resistance	Costly to administer
Door-to-door couponing	Very selective High redemption rate	Time consuming Needs careful supervision Lead time needed

Techniques	Advantages	Disadvantages
Direct-mail couponing	High targetability At home coverage High redemption rate	Needed Costly Dependent upon list quality
Newspaper couponing	Quick and convenient Geographically targetable Low cost	Low redemption rate Retailers may balk Requires careful planning
Magazine/supplement couponing	Targeted audience Effective coverage Increases in readership	Can become expensive Consumers neglect to clip Slow redemption rate
Money refund	Generates new business Reinforces brand loyalty	Results can be slow Modest impact
In-or-near pack premiums	Increases product sales Modest distribution cost	Bonus to loyal buyers Pilferage problem
Self-liquidating premiums	Low cost Boosts brand image	Modest sales impact May be too popular
Price pack	Moves merchandise Keeps up visibility	Not selective May cheapen brand image
Contests/sweepstakes	No purchase required Increases brand awareness	Expensive Modest participation
Trading stamps/ promotional games	No extra expense for consumer Creates store preference	Consumer boredom Expensive
Point-of-purchase displays	Effective stimulation	Requires dealer cooperation

Table 8.2: Advantages and disadvantages of various sales promotion techniques

Develop your sales promotion program

Having selected the techniques most suitable for accomplishing your objectives for one or more of your prospective audiences – salesforce, dealers, and consumers – you must now work out the operational details of your campaign. This activity includes determining the budget for your program, which has to take into account three types of costs:

1. The *administrative cost*, covering creative aspects, production of the promotional material, mailing, and advertising.

How to manage your communications strategy

eight

2. The *incentive cost,* which includes the cost of the premium, coupon, price pack, and salesforce or dealer incentive and reflects, of course, the likely rate of redemption (which can vary greatly, depending upon the method of delivery).

3. The *marginal product cost,* such as the cost of a different package or imprint, or of overtime or supplementary purchases required by the temporary increase in output.

Of necessity, the budget for a specific campaign will be set according to the promotional needs of the product during the remainder of the year, as well as the needs of other elements of the product mix. Also, the specific budget is bound by the size of the overall annual appropriation for sales promotion, which is usually spelled out as a *percentage of a company's advertising and sales promotion budget* and may run anywhere from 20% for business-to-business firms to 60% for consumer goods.

When deciding on the length of your campaign, you will find yourself at a critical point. If the promotion is too short, neither you nor your target audience will derive sufficient benefit from it. On the other hand, if it is too long, your brand's image is likely to be cheapened and your campaign's 'act now' urgency will be diluted.

A related issue is, of course, frequency – that is, how often you should promote a given product. Generally, the rules are not too often, not too short, and not too long.

Pretest your sales promotion programme

Having further determined when to run your campaign, make sure your schedule ties in smoothly with the other elements of your marketing plan as well as with the plans of your purchasing and production departments. You should now proceed to pretest your campaign on a limited scale. This activity will help to reassure you that you have chosen the most appropriate device and incentive, and are delivering it in the most effective manner.

Implement and evaluate your campaign

Once your campaign has been fine-tuned and fully orchestrated, you can put it into effect. If you are introducing a new product, you may want to demonstrate it at a national sales meeting to motivate your salesforce to go out and excel. For an established product, you may instead send your salespeople kits that spell out the campaign objectives and its operational details, as well as the nature and size of the incentives offered to them, your dealers, and your consumers.

It will be helpful to equip your salespeople with audiovisual aids and samples of the promotional materials. They also need persuasive arguments to support their efforts, and a schedule specifying start-up dates, advertising support, and expiration of the deal. A well-informed, enthusiastic salesforce is vital to the success of your program.

As an astute manager you should monitor the progress of your campaign closely and continually. Poor execution can cause it to back-fire by creating frustration and ill will. Therefore, make every effort to achieve the objectives of your campaign.

You can measure the extent of campaign effectiveness in various ways. The essential ones, for example, are in the form of product movement or market-share figures. It is here that you must keep in mind the limitations of your sales promotion campaign, namely: *Sales promotion is a short-term tool that can support long-term goals only in a supplementary capacity.* It cannot build a consumer franchise.

To the contrary, if it is used too often it can destroy the image of a brand. Thus, it should be used not as a substitute for advertising, but rather as a complementary effort.

Marketing over the Internet

From retailers to brokers to manufacturers, the pervasive use of the Internet has transformed the way individuals buy and the methods by which companies conduct business. Its usage is as far-reaching as the World Wide Web itself, with applications as sweeping as trading stocks, obtaining information on autos, subscribing to book and music clubs, getting price quotes on mortgages, and purchasing airline tickets.

Further, marketers are using the Internet with greater precision to do specific jobs, such as: acquire customers,cultivate brand aware-ness, and open new markets. Other uses include: Product penetration, research, and positioning the company as a leader. To match those goals, budgets for the Internet continue to increase, usually at the expense of other media.

Many organizations are adapting to the explosive use of the Internet. For example:

- **Hewett-Packard Co**. uses the Internet to track how their customers consume business information. Based on the feedback, HP made a fairly significant shift from traditional broadcast and print advertising to online marketing. Also, by paying close attention to evolving technology and the trends in communicating, the company regularly uses webcasts, online video, blogs, podcasts, and online communities to launch new products and develop ongoing relationships with customers.

- **Government Computer Sales**, a hardware and software-procurement service, has created a profile of 3,400 government departments according to on-line and traditional sales. The profiles help the company conduct 60% of its interactions on-line, as well as track buyer behaviour to reach those customers who buy with the greatest frequency. That precise targeting has helped GCS tailor its communications to convince its clients, on average, to nearly double the number of software programs and computer products they buy.

- **Consolidated Freightways**, a trucking company, found a way to cater to small businesses. When visitors click on its website to look at specific rate quotes, a window pops up offering on-line help. While customers get rapid information, Consolidated also collects valuable data from them that, in turn, it uses to solicit additional business at relatively low cost.

- **PIMCO Funds**, an investment-advisory firm, offers an Internet service that uses each investor profile to tailor a proposed investment portfolio within two minutes after receiving the information. About 30 daily proposals are now being generated from the system. PIMCO estimates that if half the proposals are accepted, this will add 75% more business than it would have gained from other marketing efforts.

- **BabyCenter Inc**. is a leading operator of Web sites targeting parents of infants and young children. Its BabyCenter.com, ParentCenter.com, and BabyCentre.co.uk sites attract more than 3 million people with articles on childcare, health, and nutrition, as well as information for single parents, balancing work and family issues, and education. The sites also offer online stores featuring clothing and furniture for infants and children, along with toys, books, and associated products.

To be more specific about the impressive workings of the Internet, let's track a particular transaction where a computer maker is searching for the best price and delivery of a memory chip in an open-market networking system:

1. A computer maker needs 10,000 memory chips to assemble one of its new models.

2. The purchasing department logs on to the Internet network and enters specifications about the chip. The system shows a list of available chips with price, quantity, and other data.

3. The computer maker puts in a price. E-mail notifies the suppliers and other buyers interested in the same part of the bid.

4. The seller indicates its selling price. The buyer is alerted by e-mail and accepts the price.

What the above example illustrates is the workings of Internet bidding exchanges for a wide array of products to connect buyers and sellers in both business-to-consumer and business-to-business transactions.

The ability to utilize the Internet is not confined to large organizations, small companies with limited sales resources can establish a home page as a way to communicate a product message, offer special deals, announce a new service, or launch into foreign markets.

Regardless of company size, follow these guidelines to make the Internet work for you:

1. Register a 'domain name'. A domain name uses the familiar format of *www.yourcompany.com*. The name is an address that establishes an Internet presence. Numerous website marketing services exist to help you register a domain name.

2. As indicated in the above examples, utilize e-mail to develop a dialogue between buyer and seller. E-mail can distribute information, survey customers, update prices, develop a quote bidding system, and close the sale.

3. Establish 'links' or electronic connections to tie your own and non-competing web sites. This helps build an inexpensive on-line referral network that attracts customers with common interests in both companies.

4. Offer genuine information that is useful and applicable to customers and prospects. The object is to follow the marketing-driven approach of solving customers' problems and forming

long-term relationships. Such information might indicate new applications of your product, a diagnostic menu for solving the most common operating problems, or providing training materials to hone customers' skills.

Having established your Internet presence, the next step is to market your on-line service and have customers and prospects visit your site. The following guidelines will assist you in gaining visibility:

- Promote your website in all advertising media, including sales promotion brochures, technical manuals, letterheads, and business cards.

- Display your web address on packages, in-store displays, and counter tops.

- Use your web address on press releases and any articles written for or about your firm.

- Develop dedicated promotions that 'sell' the recipient on the advantages of visiting your web site. This goes together with the guideline of offering genuine information to the visitor.

- Register with web search engines, the means by which individuals locate sites that interest them. You can also buy a banner ad in a popular search engine in a particular section in which your company is classified. Interested users can then link or connect to your site, thereby increasing your traffic at a modest cost.

This exciting promotion medium is still relatively in its infancy and with the revenue growth in the 21st century projected to skyrocket into the billions, establishing a solid presence on the Internet will pay off in sales growth and market expansion. The bottom-line: Make the Internet an integral component of your promotion plan.

Best practices

Speed is the essence of promotional success. There are few cases, if any, of a profitable campaign that was prolonged. A campaign may lack ingenuity, but it has a chance for success if delivered with extraordinary speed.

Effective use of promotion can force competitors to react to your moves on your terms. For example, the timing of your promotion can weaken competitors by making them use additional resources after they have completed a major sales promotion effort.

To identify communications strategies and initiate action:

1. List the advertising, sales promotion, and Internet objectives that represent the best opportunities and then integrate them into your marketing mix (product, price, promotion, and distribution).

2. Prioritize those strategies for implementation and identify those individuals who are assigned the tasks.

3. Monitor results and fine-tune your objectives and strategies to achieve the desired results.

4. Make necessary changes in your strategic marketing plan, so that you can maintain overall direction of your marketing efforts.

9

How to manage your pricing strategy

Chapter objectives

Sales forecasting

Pricing new products

Pricing strategies

Pricing established products

Pricing guidelines

Best practices

Chapter objectives

After reading this chapter, you should be able to:

- Use sales forecasting techniques to devise pricing strategies.
- Apply the five pricing strategy options for new products.
- Apply the six pricing strategy applications for established products.
- Initiate the steps to convert pricing strategies into action.

Although pricing a product or service follows a specific process, you should be attentive to the following broad guidelines when devising a strategy:

- First, do not isolate pricing from the other parts of the marketing mix (product, promotion, and distribution).
- Second, take into account your company's goals. Give thoughtful attention to your management's views on market share, return on investment, ability to compete with larger or more aggressive competitors, and the stage your product in is in its life cycle (introduction, growth, maturity, or phase-out).
- Third, when faced with tough price competition and before you get involved in pricing wars, examine all possible alternatives, such as product differentiation, service improvement, promotion innovation, and supply chain strategies.

In addition to the above broad guidelines, there is one preliminary step in the pricing process: forecasting sales potential. Shaping a sales forecast provides a pragmatic framework for measuring the financial impact of your pricing strategies.

Sales forecasting

Forecasting furnishes a set of alternative sales potentials derived from various market scenarios. You can use these sales potentials as a frame of reference in assessing your marketing opportunities and evaluating the payoffs of your marketing strategies under a variety of conditions.

You can then deploy company resources to take full advantage of the opportunities open to you. The outcome of this process is your sales forecast.

Thus, sales forecasting is an organized effort to predict the future level of sales, given specific marketing strategies and particular assumptions about market conditions. You get under way by examining past events and developments, as well as making use of your present knowledge and experience to project future sales possibilities.

However, merely projecting past figures into the future as if they were isolated from events is not sales forecasting. You need to combine objective, factual inputs with subjective judgment.

Judgment is essential for meaningful sales forecasts. In fact, forecasts are typically generated in cycles. That is, they are made, refined, and then revised. These cycles are repeatedly run through until, in the opinion of the forecaster, the optimum combination of marketing strategy and sales results occurs.

A well-managed forecasting program will make projections in time to allow corrective measures, not when developments are too far-gone. Such a program can also provide you with frequent comparisons of actual-to-forecast figures so you can revise your pricing tactics during the forecast period.

No forecast should ever be allowed to go unmonitored or become outdated. Instead, it should be used as a powerful tool to develop meaningful pricing strategies for both new and established products.

Sales forecasting techniques

Fortunately, sales forecasting methods are not mutually exclusive. Actually, it is advisable to use multiple approaches for arriving at estimated sales. If they all yield similar results, you can place great confidence in your figures.

If, however, they diverge widely, you should find out why and reconcile them before a commitment is made. Using a multiple-method procedure acts as a system of checks and balances, assuring you of meaningful composite predictions.

Although various computer models are available to do sales forecasts, time and budget restrictions often bar their use. Rather, executives often rely on a set of relatively simple, quick, do-it-yourself techniques that substantially reduce the time and money required in forecasting.

There are a number of such forecasting techniques that, along with subjective judgment, add precision to sales estimates. These consist of non-mathematical forecasting techniques that are subdivided into:

- Judgmental methods, involving the opinions of various kinds of experts such as executives, salespeople, and informed outsiders.

- Market surveys using buyer surveys and market tests.

Judgmental methods

Judgment from the extremes

Judgment from the extremes entails asking for an expert's opinion as to whether or not future sales are likely to be at an extremely high or extremely low level. If the expert's reaction is that neither seems probable, the range between the extremes is successively reduced until an approximate level of expected sales is reached. Resulting in a range rather than a single figure estimate, this approach is appropriate in situations where experts feel incapable of giving one-level forecasts.

Group discussion method

The accuracy of a forecast hinges heavily on the ability of the expert(s) to produce realistic estimates. As a quick check on figures, the judgment-from-the-extremes approach proves very useful. However, the forecaster often feels that a team of knowledgeable individuals should be invited to participate in forecasting.

Most often, such a team meets as a committee and comes up with a group estimate through consensus. This group discussion method has the advantage of merging divergent viewpoints and moderating individual biases.

You should, however, guard against the potential disadvantage of one or more individual dominating the discussion. Also, be alert to superficial responses by those who lack individual responsibility for pricing and are unwilling to participate actively in the process.

Pooled individual estimates method

While the pooled individual estimates method avoids the potential pitfalls of group discussions, it also lacks the benefits of group dynamics. A project leader simply merges separately supplied estimates into a single estimate, without any interplay with or between the participants.

Delphi technique

A popular method for forecasting is the Delphi technique, which overcomes the drawbacks of both group discussion and pooled individual estimates methods. In this approach, group members are asked to submit individual estimates and assumptions.

These are reviewed by the project leader, revised, and fed back to the participants for a second round. Participants are also informed of the median forecast level that emerged from the previous round.

Domination, undue conservatism, and argument are eliminated because of the written, rather than oral, procedure and the group members benefit from one another's input. After successive rounds of estimating and feedback, the process ends when a consensus emerges.

Jury of executive opinion

The experts consulted in one or more of these methods are typically recruited from one of three pools: executives, salespeople, and informed outsiders. A jury of executive opinion is often composed of top-level personnel from various key functions such as sales, production, and finance. The major advantage of this type of source is that forecasts can be arrived at quickly.

This advantage is, however, easily outweighed by the disadvantage inherent in involving people in the estimating process who, in spite of their high rank, are relatively unfamiliar with the grassroots forces that shape market success.

Composite of salesforce opinion

The composite of salesforce opinion approach collects product, customer, and/or territorial estimates from individual salespeople in the field. Since they are in constant contact with customers, salespeople should be in a position to predict buying plans and needs. They may even be able to take into account probable competitive activity.

Salespeople who call on relatively few industrial accounts and work very closely with them are likely to produce the best forecasts. Conversely, salespeople who call on many accounts in visits that are widely spaced will be of relatively little help in predicting sales.

Few companies simply add up their salesforce's estimates to compute the sales forecast. Since sales quotas are frequently based on these estimates, a salesperson will tend to be conservative or pessimistic in estimating sales. This tendency is partially corrected by rewarding accuracy and distributing records showing the accuracy of past forecasts. Or management can allocate promotional support to a territory in line with the sales estimate (in which case it may, of course, become a self-fulfiling prophecy).

To counter the additional problem that many salespeople are unfamiliar with broad economic trends, many firms supply their salespeople with basic assumptions to guide their estimates. In spite of its drawbacks, the effort may well be worth it. For one thing, morale is likely to be higher if salespeople have had a hand in their own forecasts and quotas.

Outside experts

When it comes to outside experts, any knowledgeable source could be consulted – for example, trade associations or economists. Marketing researchers are another valuable resource, together with dealers and distributors. However, it is generally difficult to assess the degree of familiarity with industry conditions and trends of such outsiders. Thus, they should be used with caution and only in a supplementary capacity.

Market survey

Consumer surveys

The judgmental methods just described involve estimates by people who are not themselves the ultimate buyers. Some observers consider this fact a weakness and suggest getting the word directly from 'the horse's mouth'.

Surveys of consumer buying intentions are particularly appropriate when past trends (such as energy consumption) are unlikely to continue and/or historical data (as for a new product or market) does not exist.

This technique works best for major consumer durables and industrial capital expenditures, since these types of buying decisions require a considerable amount of planning and lead time, and the respondents are able to predict their own behaviour with reasonable accuracy.

However, where some types of consumer purchases are not planned sufficiently in advance, these estimates end up as guesses. Also, a substantial bias may be involved because interviewees might want to please the interviewer, or might give an arbitrary answer because they cannot predict their own behaviour in an unfamiliar situation.

In addition to the possible drawback that prospective purchasers might be unwilling to disclose their intentions, it should be remembered that answers given refer to future, and thus hypothetical behaviour, rather than actual behaviour.

Test marketing

The problem of accuracy can be remedied by using the test marketing approach whereby a new product, or a variation in the marketing mix for an established one, is introduced in a limited number of test locations. That is, the entire marketing programme that is scheduled on a national basis is put into effect, scaled down to the local level, but otherwise identical in every detail, including advertising, pricing, packaging, etc.

The new marketing effort now has to compete in a real sales environment. Purchases, if any, are actual, not hypothetical. If carefully chosen and monitored, test markets can provide a significant mini-picture of the full-scale reaction to the planned change. On the basis of actual sales results in the test markets, sales forecasts are simply scaled up by appropriate factors.

Table 9.1 summarizes the methods discussed.

METHOD	NATURE	BENEFITS	DRAWBACKS
Judgmental			
Judgment from the extremes	Successive narrowing of high-low range	Range instead of single figure	Depends on individual estimating
Group discussion	Group consensus estimate	Merges divergent views, moderate biases	Domination by one individual, superficiality
Pooled and individual estimates	Averaging of individual estimates	Avoids group discussion pitfalls	Lacks group dynamics
Delphi technique	Successive written rounds of estimating with feedback from other participants	Eliminates domination, conservatism, superficial response	Lacks group dynamics
Jury of executive opinion	Top-level committee	Rapid response	Unfamiliar with market conditions
Composite of sales force opinion	Adjusted estimates from individual salespeople	Front-line expertise, motivational tool	Bias due to impact on compensation, unfamiliar with economic trends
Outside experts	Merging of outside opinions	No bias due to personal interests	Difficult to assess degree of expertise
Market surveys			
Consumer surveys	Consumer interviews about buying intentions	Directly from users	Hypothetical behaviour
Test marketing	Sale in limited number of locations	Actual sales results	Costly, time-consuming, exposes strategy to competitors

Table 9.1: Comparison of non-mathematical forecasting methods

With sales forecasts established, you are now in a qualified position to address pricing strategies. What follows is detailed information you can use to select strategies for both new and existing products.

Pricing new products

With the launch of new products, skimming a market with high prices, penetrating with low prices, using odd or even prices, or following the market leader are strategies determined by a wide range of factors. Such factors include:

- Market share and competitive position.

- Product image.

- Speed of market entry.

- Time needed to recover your investment.

- How far behind competition is with a similar product entry.

To introduce you to pricing strategies, consider the following case of a company that had to deal with offshore competitors selling into its market with prices 30% to 40% below overall market prices.

Cummins

The heavy-duty diesel engine manufacturer, Cummins, had been fighting aggressively against two formidable Japanese competitors: Komatsu and Nissan. The first word of a problem came from Cummins' customers, Navistar and Freightliner. Both companies reported they had been testing Japanese medium-sized diesel truck engines.

Knowing the Japanese strategy of using an indirect approach into a market, Cummins saw the medium engine as a strategic threat. The entry could lead to the next step of penetrating Cummins' 30% share of the North American market for heavy-duty diesel truck engines.

Cummins managers saw the Japanese competitors' strategy evolve:

- They entered the market with prices 40% below prevailing levels to buy market share fast.

- They found a poorly served and emerging market segment in medium-sized engines through which to enter.

- They developed a quality product and were prepared to expand their product lines.

Faced with the problem, Cummins managers took the following actions:

1. They launched into the medium-sized truck engine market with four new engine models. This timing, however, was coincidental. Cummins had been planning this market entry for five

years through a joint venture with J.I. Case, a farm machinery producer that used medium-sized diesel engines.

2. Cummins immediately cut the price of the engines to the Japanese level. As management observed, 'If you don't give the Japanese a major price advantage, they can't get in.'

3. Cummins cut costs by one-third. This action was the toughest job in what was perceived as a bare-bones efficient manu-facturing operation. Using more flexible machinery and cutting excess inventory from a 60-day supply to a 4-day supply reduced overhead.

4. Cummins managers gained participation from suppliers on suggestions about cost cutting. The result: lowering of mate-rial costs by 18%. This impressive reduction was achieved by changing the traditional adversarial attitude toward suppliers to one of fostering cooperative relationships.

The strategy worked as an effective defence, particularly as it related to Cummins' concern about its heavy-duty diesel business.

Action strategy

What can you learn from the Cummins case? A number of strategy lessons come out of the situation:

First, there are options open to you against a price attack. You observed some of those actions above. But the action must begin with a mental attitude of 'fighting back' and not giving up valuable market share without a battle.

Second, consider innovative strategies in such areas as:

*   Customer service
*   Improved delivery time
*   Extended warranties
*   Sales terms
*   After-sales support
*   Packaging
*   Management training.

Or consider innovative strategies in such intangible areas as:

*   Reliability
*   Image

- Nice-to-do-business-with reputation
- Credibility
- Prestige
- Convenience
- Value
- Responsiveness to problems
- Access to key individuals in your firm.

Lessons

The primary message of the Cummins example is that pricing strategy is never derived in isolation of other components of the marketing mix. Another major consideration is how pricing affects the product's image in the customer's mind. Cummins built and maintained a solid market image through product quality, innovation, and best-in-class service.

When pricing new products in your line, you must ask:

- Can low price and high price be compatible?
- Do you create a conflict in the customer's mind?
- What perception or image do customers hold in their minds about your product?

Give careful consideration to these questions when positioning a product into a new category and devising a pricing strategy counter to traditional patterns. Some organizations recognize image as a precious factor and will create a new name brand within a low-price category, for example, to avoid conflict rather than run the risk of damaging the image of its upscale product.

In general, it is difficult to regain a premium price position for the same brand once it has been diluted by low price promotions through mass merchandizing outlets. Therefore, as you shape a strategy for a new product entry, it is wise to maintain ongoing feedback about the market position you want. In turn, the market position you select ultimately has consequences on your product's image.

Pricing strategies

Skim pricing

The first of the strategies that deal with new products is skim pricing. This involves pricing at a high level to hit the 'cream' of the buyers who are less sensitive to price. The conditions for weighing this strategy are:

- Senior management requires that you recover R&D, equipment, technology and other start-up costs rapidly.

- The product or service is unique. It is new (or improved) and in the introductory stage of the product life cycle. Or the product serves a relatively small segment where price is not a major consideration.

- There is little danger of short-term competitive entry because of patent protection, high R&D entry costs, high promotion costs, or limitations on availability of raw materials, or because major distribution channels are filled.

- There is a need to control demand until production is geared up.

The electronics industry usually employs skim pricing at the introductory stage of the product life cycle to the point that consumers and industrial buyers expect the high introductory-pricing pattern. There are exceptions, however.

One was Texas Instruments' introduction of its much-touted solid state magnetic storage device for computers that had the capability of not losing stored data when power was cut off. Even with the impressive technology, sales were initially disappointing because potential users were not willing to pay the high introductory price and were willing to wait for price reductions.

Penetration pricing

Penetration pricing means pricing below the prevailing level in order to gain market entry or to increase market share. The conditions for considering this strategy are:

- There is an opportunity to establish a quick foothold in a specific market.

- Existing competitors are not expected to react to your prices.

- The product or service is a 'me too' entry and you have achieved a low-cost producer capability.

- You hold to the theory that high market share equals high return on investment, and management is willing to wait for the rewards.

One of the most striking examples of penetration pricing occurred in the fast-growing market for computer printers. Initially, during the early stages of the product life cycle, the Japanese seized the opportunity and targeted the low-priced segment for printers.

Such companies as Ricoh, Okidata, Shinshu, and Seiki attacked the segment by offering printers at rock-bottom prices and short delivery times. From virtually no sales, the Japanese secured 75% of all units selling for less than $500.

Psychological pricing

Psychological pricing means pricing at a level that is perceived to be much lower than it actually is: $99, $49, $19.99, and $0.99. Psychological pricing is a viable strategy and you should experiment with it to determine its precise application for your product. The conditions for considering this strategy are:

- A product is singled out for special promotion.

- A product is likely to be advertised, displayed, or quoted in writing.

- The selling price desired is close to a multiple of 10, 100, 1,000, etc.

While psychological pricing is most likely to be applied to consumer products, there is an increasing use of the strategy for business-to-business products and services, as in the example of a machine priced at $29,237.00.

As a further example of the psychological effect of pricing, in instances where a prestige product or service is offered, a psychological price may be expressed as 'one hundred dollars', therefore giving an elitist impression.

Follow pricing

Pricing in relation to industry price leaders is termed follow pricing. The conditions for considering this strategy are:

- Your organization may be a small or medium-sized company in an industry dominated by one or two price leaders.

- Aggressive pricing fluctuations may result in damaging price wars.

- Most products offered don't have distinguishing features.

IBM traditionally set the pricing standards by which its competitors priced their products. However, this situation turned out to be a two-edged sword.

When clones, primarily from China, priced products and services at 20% to 40% below IBM's levels, IBM was forced to reverse its role and use follow pricing against aggressive competitors for some of its product lines as a means of protecting its share of the market. Yet, IBM's use of follow pricing was a holding action in its broader strategy of attempting to regain leadership with the introduction of cutting-edge new products, with an emphasis on unique services and systems.

Cost-plus pricing

Cost-plus pricing entails basing price on product costs and then adding on components such as administration and profit. The conditions for using this strategy are:

- The pricing procedure conforms to government, military, or construction regulations.

- There are unpredictable total costs owing to ongoing new product development and testing phases.

- A project (product) moves through a series of start-and-stop sequences.

Cost-plus pricing, unless mandated by government procedures, is product-based pricing. Such an approach contrasts with market-based pricing, which takes into consideration such internal and external factors as:

- Corporate, divisional, or product-line objectives concerning profits, competitive inroads, market share, and market stability.

- Target-market objectives dealing with desired market position, profile of customer segments, current demand for product, and future potential of the market.

- Marketing mix strategy; for example, how pricing fits together with product, promotion, and distribution components of the mix.

Pricing established products

You can avoid or postpone price wars by locating untapped market segments and focusing on product improvements. You can also pre-empt and discourage new competitors by gradually sliding down prices, thereby making the market seem unprofitable. You can always price according to the flexibility of demand and your production economies.

The following case illustrates a pricing strategy in a highly competitive arena where market share and profitability are the major issues.

Intel Corp.

The large maker of computer chips, Intel Corp., has been dealing successfully with a multifaceted problem:

- First, it has been battling aggressive high-profile competitors such as Advanced Micro Devices and National Semiconductor that were looking to unseat the market leader.

- Second, it has operated in a market where average PC prices dropped over 7% during a 12-month period.

- Third, it has attempted to build market share while tackling the formidable task of preserving profitability.

Intel's strategy

Intel management crafted a well-balanced strategy that harmonized with the needs of the customers, the actions of energetic competitors, and the internal workings of the Intel organization.

The essence of Intel's strategy focused on the following:

- Management wisely decided to segment its product line into chips aimed at specific markets, such as inexpensive PCs, mid-tier 'performance' PCs, and powerful corporate servers. Doing so allowed Intel to balance thin profits from products like the low-end Celeron with high-profit items such as the powerful Pentium chips.

- To add a measure of security to the above action, Intel mounted an unprecedented cost-cutting program to keep profits on track. For example, it accelerated its move to next-generation chip manufacturing technology which promises to dramatically slash its unit costs. Instead of buying all-new production gear, the company plans to reuse 70% of its current equipment as it shifts to the new chips. Other cost-cutting approaches included curtailing travel spending by using more videoconferencing and reducing staff through attrition and layoffs.

207

- Intel pushed forward on product improvement by recasting the Celeron chip and aggressively springing for market share by introducing faster models in a bid to gain market share in high-profit servers and workstations.

- The company beefed up overseas marketing in places such as China, India, and Latin America. With a concerted effort to stabilize prices while maintaining profitability, Intel urged customers to place their orders over the Internet, which reduced processing expenses and improved productivity.

The Intel case illustrates the external and internal considerations that go into the selection of pricing strategies. Once those issues are addressed, you can then deal with the actual selection of a strategy. For established products, begin with the following:

Slide-down pricing

The first in this series of strategies is slide-down pricing. The aim is to move prices down to tap successive layers of demand. The conditions for considering this strategy are:

- The product would appeal to progressively larger groups of users at lower prices in a price-elastic market.

- The organization has adopted a low-cost producer strategy by adhering to learning curve concepts (costs decrease as experience increases) and other economies of scale in distribution, promotion, and sales.

- There is a need to discourage competitive entries.

Slide-down pricing is best utilized in a proactive management mode rather than as a reaction to competitors' pressures. If you anticipate the price movements and do sufficient segmentation analysis to identify price-sensitive groups, you can target those groups with specific promotions to pre-empt competitors' actions.

Whereas skim pricing begins with high pricing, it evolves to slide-down pricing. The downward movement of price usually coincides with such events as new competitors entering to buy market share through low price and then waits for economies of scale to take effect.

Segment pricing

Segment pricing involves pricing essentially the same products differently to various groups. The conditions for considering this strategy are:

- The product is appropriate for several market segments.

- If necessary, the product can be modified or packaged at minimal costs to fit the varying needs of customer groups.

- The consuming segments are non-competitive and do not violate legal constraints.

Examples of segment pricing abound. The most visible ones are airlines that offer essentially one product, an airplane seat between two destinations. Yet this 'same' product may serve different segments, such as business people, clergy, students, military, senior citizens, each at different prices. Then, there is further segmentation according to time of day, day of the week, or length of stay at one destination.

To best take advantage of this pricing strategy, search out poorly served, unserved, or emerging market segments.

Flexible pricing

Pricing to meet competitive or marketplace conditions is known as flexible pricing. The conditions for considering this strategy are:

- There is a competitive challenge from imports.

- Pricing variations are needed to create tactical surprise and break predictable patterns.

- There is a need for fast reaction against competitors attacking your market with penetration pricing.

The previously cited case of Cummins illustrates how that company used flexible pricing as part of its strategy to counterattack the Japanese manufacturers moving in on its diesel engine market. Cummins' management deliberately lowered prices to blunt the penetrating pricing attacks of the Japanese engine entries.

As organizations downsize and re-engineer to become more competitive, typically field managers who are closer to the dynamics of the market are handed greater pricing authority and accountability for their products. The intent is to allow a flexible pricing strategy when appropriate.

In contrast, the opportunity to react is missed where there is a long chain of command from field managers to executive levels, with the detrimental effect of consuming excessive response time.

It is necessary for middle managers to identify competitive situations where flexible pricing may be used. However, you should remember that flexible pricing, as in all applications of pricing strategy, is not a licence to reduce prices to meet competitors' levels in all circumstances. Pricing is still but one component of the marketing mix and you should view it within that total framework of marketing strategy options.

Pre-emptive pricing

Pre-emptive pricing is used to discourage competitive market entry. The conditions for considering this strategy are:

- You hold a strong position in a medium to small market.

- You have sufficient coverage of the market and sustained customer loyalty (that is, customer satisfaction) to cause competitors to view the market as unattractive.

Again referring to Cummins, management used pre-emptive pricing to protect its dominant position in the diesel engine market when it cut prices to block competitive entry. Pre-emptive pricing, as with flexible pricing, requires close contact with the field. Customers, competitors, market and economic conditions, and any other factors could influence pricing decisions.

Phase-out pricing

Phase-out pricing means pricing high to remove a product from the line. The conditions for considering this strategy are:

- The product has entered the down side of the product life cycle, but it is still used by a few customers.

- Sudden removal of the product from the line would create severe problems for your customers and create poor relations.

Phase-out pricing does not mean dumping a product. Rather, it is intended for use with a select group of customers who are willing to pay a higher price for the convenience of a source of supply. For example, Echlin Inc., the producer of car and truck parts, stocked nearly 150,000 different parts for every car from the Ford Model T to a Rolls Royce. Customers with old or rare car models were only too pleased to pay the price for product availability.

Loss-leader pricing

Pricing a product low to attract buyers for other products is called loss-leader pricing. The conditions for considering this strategy are:

- Complimentary products are available that can be sold in combination with the loss leader at normal price levels.

- The product is used to draw attention to a total product line and increase the customer following. The strategy is particularly useful in conjunction with impulse buying.

Loss-leader is one of the most common forms of pricing strategy. It is prevalent in all ranges of businesses, from department stores to car dealers to industrial product lines. You should remember, however, to consider the profitability of the total product line.

Pricing guidelines

Finally, use the following guidelines to increase your chances for success:

1. **Establish your pricing objectives**. These might be to maximize profits, increase sales revenues, increase market share rapidly, or position your product advantageously among competitive look-alike products.

2. **Develop a demand schedule for your product**. Specifically forecast the probable quantities purchased at various price levels.

3. **Examine competitors' pricing**. This review will determine where you can position your price to achieve your specific market objectives.

4. **Select your pricing method**. Use the strategies outlined in this chapter.

Best practices

Before converting your pricing strategies into action, remember: Price wars are like fire. Those who persist in such actions are ultimately consumed by them.

To identify strategies and initiate action:

1. List pricing strategies that represent your best opportunities and will avoid price wars.

2. Indicate what action you will take and who is assigned the task of monitoring price performance.

3. Relate feedback to the objective(s) desired and the strategies selected.

4. List immediate plans for implementing your follow-on strategy and indicate future courses of action based on various scenarios that could affect your pricing and eventually impact your profitability and market position.

10

How to manage your distribution strategy

Chapter objectives

Channel commitment

Channel coverage

Distribution and market exposure

Direct versus indirect distribution

Making the channel decision

Channel control

Selecting distributors

Evaluating distributors

Best practices

Chapter objectives

After reading this chapter, you should be able to:

- Develop the primary strategies for moving a product to its intended market.

- Explain the criteria for choosing channels of distribution.

- Identify techniques for evaluating supply chain performance.

The ultimate success of your business strategy depends on moving your product to its intended market. Accordingly, you should take considerable care in selecting supply chain strategies and considering the far-reaching impact of channel decisions.

Such decisions involve:

1. The long-term commitment to the supply chain.

2. The amount of geographic coverage needed to maintain a competitive advantage.

3. The possibility of competitive inroads.

Channel commitment

Your initial step in developing a channel strategy is to review the categories of products being sold by your company and their respective market coverage.

Consider these criteria:

- Specialty products do best with exclusive (restricted) distribution.

- Convenience products do best with intensive (widespread) distribution.

- Shopping products do best with selective (high sales potential) distribution.

Next, determine if existing channels provide adequate market coverage and if there are expansion possibilities to which you can make a commitment.

The following case illustrates one dimension of a distribution strategy:

Ryerson, Inc.

The company is a leading distributor and processor of metals. Ryerson's products include aluminum, copper, and industrial plastics. Operating within a well-managed supply chain, the company buys bulk metal products in the shape of sheets, bars, and other forms from metal producers. Then it processes them into smaller lots to meet the specifications of its customers – machine shops, fabricators, metal producers, and machinery makers.

With a seamless focus on its customers and suppliers; and with meticulous attention to the smooth flow of products throughout the supply chain, Ryerson achieved one-year (2005) sales growth of an outstanding 75.1%.

Ryerson's innovative and take-charge distribution strategy satisfies the surging demand of customers who want delivery on time, when they want it, and without the financial and physical burdens of carrying excessive inventory.

Further, by not limiting itself to domestic markets, Ryerson is exporting the same distribution model to its operations in Canada, China, and India.

Action strategy

What can you learn from the Ryerson case? If Ryerson's successful distribution strategy arouses you to check up on how your firm distributes products, then consider these factors:

1. Enhancing your present distribution network or creating a new one affords a prime opportunity to unseat a channel leader or deter a challenger. Begin by tailoring distribution to each major market segment, weighing the following alternatives:

   - **Direct versus distributors**: Whereas there may be a tendency to eliminate the middleman from the supply chain and thereby permit direct access to the end user, be certain that you can maintain the flexible response to customers' increasing demands.

   - **Distributors versus brokers**: Whereas distributors typically carry inventory and brokers do not, question how each would serve market niches in light of customers' need for critical delivery schedules, immediate customer assistance, and storage requirements.

   - **Distributors versus retailers**: Pinpoint how each of these two options is efficient. Take into account quantities purchased, services rendered, and access to technical backup.

- **Exclusive versus non-exclusive outlets**: Weigh up the pros and cons. Exclusivity may constrict a channel's breadth of coverage, yet provide compensating service and commitment benefits. On the other hand, non-exclusive outlets may broaden overall availability, but impair the level of commitment required for your product line.

2. Infusing value-added services into your supply chain strategy may provide enough differentiation that will save your product from becoming a commodity. For example, consider the following value-added strategies:

   - Make use of greater mobility by following your customers into growth segments and satisfying their logistical needs.

   - Develop one-stop-shopping that allows buyers to order a variety of related products with ease, convenience, and volume discounts. The combined effect would make it harder for competitors to gain a foothold in the supply chain network.

   - Centralize the delivery of technical training, customer service, and reliable after-sales support – while providing an infrastructure from which to launch into new segments.

   - Install an Internet ordering and computer-based stocking system that links customers with your operations, thereby creating an electronic stronghold making it difficult for competitors to disengage your customers.

Channel coverage

Choosing channels of distribution

There are at least three noteworthy considerations related to distribution channel coverage:

1. It involves long-term commitments to other firms.

2. It delimits the portion of the market that you can reach.

3. It affects all other marketing decisions.

What follows are guidelines for you to use in deciding on market coverage:

1. Channel coverage involves long-term commitments to other firms

Once chosen, distribution channels typically develop a great deal of inertia against change. Your choice of a channel type associates your brand in the consumer's mind with a certain kind of store or outlet, thus creating an image that is difficult, if not impossible, to alter.

Signing up individual wholesalers or retailers often involves substantial up-front outlays. This money is usually spent for:

- Factory training of service personnel

- Workshop and field training of sales personnel

- Granting of easy terms for initial stock

- Advertising and promotional support

- Field sales support through missionary salespeople.

These and many other investments and commitments would be wasted if you were to abandon these channel partners.

Remember, too, that it would hardly sit well with the trade if you walked away from your commitments. Your channel partners also would resent and resist any infringement on their franchise by your adoption of a multiple-channel strategy for the same brand.

2. Channel coverage delimits the portion of the market that you can reach

Your selection of channel members restricts the kinds and numbers of ultimate buyers that can be reached through them, effectively cutting you off from that part of the market that does not patronize those outlets. Of course, your selection of outlets may coincide with your desired target market, in which case your neglect of the remainder of the market is deliberate.

But what if you can't attract the kinds of stores or outlets that cater to the group of consumers you wish to reach? Then you have to settle for what you can get. To avoid this trap, your product, your price, and your support must satisfy the intermediaries you want to win over.

3. Channel coverage affects all other marketing decisions

The interdependence of marketing mix decisions is most evident when choosing distribution channels. If you choose a pattern of exclusive distribution, your product often becomes a luxury item requiring a high price and high dealer margins. If, on the other hand, you go after intensive market coverage, you characterize your product as mass merchandise, which, in turn, most often necessitates a low-price policy.

Choice of advertising approaches, themes, messages, and media will vary with your product's distribution channels. Also, product and packaging design must reflect the characteristics of your chosen channels.

For instance, merchandise suited for self-service outlets has to be presented differently from goods requiring the advice and explanation of knowledgeable sales personnel. Obviously, then, channel decisions cannot be made in a vacuum, since they have repercussions on every other marketing decision you make and thus affect your entire marketing effort.

This discussion on channel coverage comes alive when viewed through the following case in which one company chose a distribution channel as its competitive weapon and how the decision influenced its long-term commitments, market reach, and internal operations.

Dell Computer Corp.

This high-flying marketer continues to rack up record revenues and profits by utilizing distribution as the driving force behind its strategy. Dell defines its distribution channel as the use of direct response marketing to penetrate the huge PC industry.

The Dell case is instructive, largely because of the dismal but erroneous predictions of industry analysts. The 'experts' initially predicted that once competitors discovered buyers turning in droves to the toll-free telephone numbers and the Internet to order hardware, they would pounce on Dell and push it out of the selling channel. Those giants also thought their vast resources and powerful brand names would entice customers away from Dell. That wishful thinking never happened.

Let's look at the major factors contributing to Dell's success:

- **Target customers**: Dell's typical customer profile revealed its buyers as knowledgeable about computers, up-to-date on new systems, and specific about the products they wanted. These customers did not need or want the hand-holding assistance provided at retail outlets.

- **Internal operations**: To accommodate to its customer profile, Dell developed flexible manufacturing techniques. These techniques enabled the company to build a customer's computer virtually to order. Using different components for each order phoned in, Dell could custom-configure computers as received. With its well-honed systems in place, Dell moved heavily into the corporate segments.

- **Cost control**: Costs are kept in line because Dell carries less inventory – 35 days worth compared with an average 110 days for leading competitors. Such flexibility allowed Dell to use its direct response expertise to introduce new (and more expensive) models faster than it could through the longer manufacturer-to-distributor-to-retailer channel.

- **Channel innovation**: Dell marketers recognize that getting comfortable with their current direct channel approach could limit expansion, especially in global markets that lack the sophisticated communications and delivery systems of North America. Still exhibiting entrepreneurial flair, managers continue to investigate new distribution concepts such as interactive kiosks and expanding Dell's presence over the Internet.

Action strategies

What can you learn from the Dell case? Dell's success illustrates channel power. Defined as the ability to set channel standards and control performance, channel power can even influence other organizations' channel decisions. For Dell, applying the power had the marketing effect of preventing the industry giants from taking control of the direct channel.

Let's examine a specific component of Dell's channel power to show its application through inventory management and control. Dell's supply management system allows it to maintain just enough inventory to satisfy customer order requirements – fast.

In turn, 'fast' translates into the now familiar just-in-time (JIT) delivery that evolved into a marketing strategy beginning in the 1980s. Demonstrated by Dell, JIT became the differentiating ingredient of its direct marketing effort and resulted in a selling advantage market leaders could not initially match.

The Dell case illustrates a number of advantages for you to consider by paying closer attention to inventory management and control as part of your distribution strategy. For example:

1. Dell built a product strategy around efficient inventory management. The capacity to store only the most widely used computer components resulted in cost control and gave marketing and sales the flexibility to use price as a tactic to undercut competition on its terms. Doing so also allowed greater control over profitability at the tactical sales level.

2. Taking advantage of Dell's flexible manufacturing systems by customizing products to customers' specifications provided marketing and sales with a leading edge in preserving a high level of customer satisfaction.

3. Using direct response marketing as its primary distribution channel permitted Dell to beat competitors to the market with technology innovations that solve technical problems, before those competitors could react. For instance, at one point in the initial introduction of Intel's Pentium chip, Dell rapidly reacted to a recall problem with replacement chips, thereby demonstrating the advantage of swift movement and management control.

4. Maintaining control of the direct response channel set up a blocking action that discouraged the industry giants from attempting to reduce Dell's channel power.

Distribution and market exposure

Adequate market coverage is interconnected to the product being promoted. Depending on the degree of market exposure desired, you can choose from exclusive, intensive, and selective distribution strategies (see Table 10.1.).

DISTRIBUTION CONSIDERATION:	1. EXCLUSIVE	2. SELECTIVE	3. INTENSIVE
Degree of coverage	Limited	Medium	Saturation
Degree of control	Stringent	Substantial	Virtually nil
Cost of distribution	Low	Medium	High
Dealer support	Substantial	Limited	Very limited
Dealer training	Extensive	Restricted	None
Type of goods	Specialty	Shopping	Convenience
Product durability	Durable	Semidurable	Nondurable
Product advertising	Yes	Yes	No
Couponing	No	No	Yes
Product example	**Automobile**	**Suit**	**Chewing gum**

Table 10.1: Considerations in choosing your degree of market exposure

Exclusive

If you sell a prestige product, you are likely to grant exclusive rights covering a geographic area to a specific wholesaler or retailer, protecting this firm against territorial encroachments by other companies carrying your products. This policy severely limits the number of middlemen handling your products and should be adopted only if you want to exercise substantial control over your intermediaries' prices, promotion, presentation, and service. It results in a stronger commitment on the part of your dealers and, thus, in a more aggressive selling effort.

Frequently practised in the automobile business, exclusive distribution, however, may lead to a number of legal problems. For instance, an exclusive dealer contract, signed between your firm and a specific retailer, prevents the middleman from selling competitors' products.

Intensive

Intensive distribution is the direct opposite of exclusivity. Popular among producers of convenience items, this policy aims to make these goods available in as many outlets as possible. As the category name suggests, buyers of such products expect them to be conveniently accessible and will not expend much shopping effort. Products in this category are frequently purchased, low-ticket non-durables, such as cigarettes and chewing gum.

Selective

Between the extremes of exclusive and intensive distribution falls selective distribution. This policy involves setting up selection criteria and deliberately restricting the number of retailers that will be permitted to handle your brand. More than one, but less than all applicants in an area will be selected. This approach implies quality without the restrictions of exclusivity.

Selective distribution is far less costly than intensive distribution and affords greater control. In particular, it is suitable for such retail goods as name-brand clothes, which fall into the semi-durables category (in contrast to the expensive durable specialty goods that are best handled through exclusive distribution).

Selective distribution lends itself to cooperative advertising, in which manufacturer and retailer share the cost.

Direct versus indirect distribution

A very basic distribution decision that you have to make relatively early in your planning is whether you want to handle the distribution of your product alone or you want to enlist expert help. The former method is called direct distribution and the latter, indirect distribution.

Direct distribution

As the name suggests, and as described in the Dell case, direct distribution involves a direct transfer of ownership from the producer to the consumer. As Figure 10.1 shows, this method does not preclude various types of facilitators from entering into the picture.

As long as they do not assume title separate and distinct from the manufacturer, the channel still remains direct. Thus, producers can sell through the mail, over the phone, door to door, via the Internet, through a factory outlet, through their own retail stores, or even through an independent agent, and still be involved in a direct transaction. Direct distribution obviously involves a greater degree of control than indirect distribution, but it cuts a producer off from the widespread coverage that the latter approach can offer.

Indirect distribution

On the other hand, indirect distribution always incorporates middlemen or resellers, who are basically of two types: wholesalers and retailers. Figure 10.1 presents a graphic comparison of the direct and indirect approaches.

What you see in Figure 10.1 is typical of the most frequently encountered channel designs. It is evident that in the direct distribution channel there is never a third party who takes title to the goods in question. For indirect distribution, the opposite situation is clearly the case, even though the manufacturer is likely to have a salesforce call on intermediaries.

The illustration does not propose to exhaust the variety of channel structures. Instead, it abstracts the most frequently used designs. As can be readily seen, multiple channels are entirely possible and are often adopted to increase exposure and impact in the marketplace.

However, selecting more than one route to the consumer can lead to competing and, at times, conflicting channels. Where it results in conflict, this distribution strategy can defeat its own purpose.

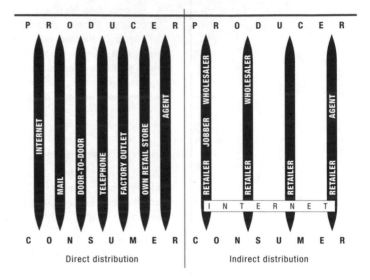

Figure 10.1: Direct and indirect distribution approaches
to alternative channel designs

The following case illustrates the workings of distribution through multiple channels with a product line that sells into both the consumer and commercial markets.

Kelly-Moore Paint Co.

A regional manufacturer of paint, Kelly-Moore Paint Co. has shown remarkable performance by producing 10% on its sales over a 10-year period, as compared with the giants Sherwin-Williams and du Pont, each of which averaged only 2.5% net on sales for the same period.

What made Kelly-Moore's success remarkable was that its primary focus was on contractors, a customer group in the supply chain that buys less than one-third of the paint sold in its marketplace.

The essence of Kelly-Moore's strategies can be summarized as follows:

> 1. It provided maximum service to contractors who generally worked out of their homes. For example, Kelly-Moore's paint stores served as free warehouse space for the contractors who could not buy paint in any volume.

2. It maintained ongoing market intelligence. Because the stores doubled as contractor warehouses, Kelly-Moore knew exactly what customers' usage and colour patterns were at any given time. Such feedback made for tighter corporate planning and helped in anticipating the changing needs and wants of the marketplace.

3. Kelly-Moore moved further down the distribution chain into the consumer end of the business by building on its contractor base. For example, when contractors left touch-up cans behind them after completing a job, Kelly-Moore used those samples to sell to consumers directly. The approach was complementary, not conflicting, since the direct-to-consumer sales were generally for the do-it-yourself segment of the market.

Action strategy

What can you learn from the Kelly-Moore case? In contrast to the Dell situation, there are a number of compelling reasons for using middlemen. The majority of manufacturers lack the financial wherewithal to perform effectively at both levels: production and distribution. They have to rely on middlemen to provide the financing for an aggressive, widespread selling effort.

Yet, even companies with adequate financial means might find investment in vertically integrated channels unattractive because of a relatively low return on investment. Thus, they might pursue higher yielding opportunities at the production end, leaving the distribution function to specialists.

Finally, producers going into the distribution business themselves often find that they must carry complementary products of other manufacturers to help defray the high cost of distribution and get maximum yield from their effort.

Making the channel decision

When the time comes to make the channel decision for your product, you should consider several factors. At first, an important consideration is: Where does the customer expect to find your product or service?

Therefore, the industry's prevailing distribution pattern is a powerful guide in making such a channel decision. If your current salesforce has related experience and appropriate business contacts, you may want to follow established routes.

Guidelines you should use when making a supply chain decision include the following:

- Companies that are strong financially have the option of direct distribution (such as Dell), while weaker firms most often need middlemen.

- If your product line is broad, you are in a better position than a specialized supplier to consider going direct. And, in keeping with marketing's credo of staying close to the customer, the fewer intermediaries you will want to have.

- You are better off going direct when you have a limited number of prospects. If they are concentrated in only a few areas, you can send out your own salesforce to make the sale.

- Should customers buy often and in small quantities, you had better let others handle the selling. Or, as an increasing number of firms do, encourage customers to use the Internet.

- Channel members are a vital link in your effort to satisfy distant customers. Therefore, by making them your partners and serving their best interests, you will find that they will help you achieve your goals.

The Internet

As discussed in other chapters of this desktop guide, there is still another factor that is making a significant impact on channel-related decisions: the Internet.

Buying electronically isn't new to many companies that have been using an older technology called Electronic Data Interchange, or EDI. But that technology is rather costly and difficult to set up.

The Internet, on the other hand, lets you not only consummate a sale, but permits quick and inexpensive transfer of all kinds of data: sales contacts, product literature, and even engineering drawings.

As a channel of distribution, doing business via the Internet shows cost savings in the range of 5% to 10% of sales – an average based on the experiences of a wide variety of companies. In more dramatic numbers, some companies reported huge advantages from on-line business relationships. For example:

- Chipmaker National Semiconductor Corp. reported saving its distributors $24 million in one year.

- Aircraft maker Boeing Co. booked $122 million in spare parts orders from airlines in one year through its websites.

- Networking giant Cisco Systems reported during the course of one year receiving $14 million in orders per day from resellers on its website.

Channel control

Channel control considers four sets of circumstances that dictate the search for new distributors:

1. New marketing plan that calls for introducing a new product line and/or entering a new market.

2. Need to intensify market coverage.

3. Need to replace existing distributors due to poor performance.

4. Industry changes or technology advances in the methods of distribution.

The distributor can be one of the key success factors in a strategy. After you've developed a channel control strategy that involves distributors, you need to know how to select and evaluate them.

Selecting distributors

Given the high degree of specialization found among distributors, your firm's management must decide how selective or comprehensive it wants to be in its market coverage. Only with the appropriate distribution mix can you satisfactorily achieve your company's marketing goals.

Your distributors will perform as you expect only if you carefully manage and constantly update your relationship with them. Therefore, develop and consistently apply well-thought-out criteria for selecting the right distribution partner in a given area.

Use the following guidelines when considering new distributors:

- As you introduce new products, you may find that your current distributors are ill equipped to sell and service them, or they handle competitive products from other manufacturers. Or, you may be addressing a new kind of clientele not serviced by your current network of distributors.

- If you enter into new geographic markets, the need for appropriate representation may become self-evident. To help determine how many and what kinds of distributors you need for a particular territory, and to facilitate the selection process, you will want to conduct a market analysis to estimate its sales potential. Rarely do you have to choose a completely new set of distributors. Your own firm's present distributors can adequately handle most new product innovations.

- As you review your share of the business in a given segment, you may conclude that your firm is under-represented. Or you may determine that your present outlets are not going after the business aggressively enough to satisfy you. As a result, you need to add more distributors in the territory, based on population, sales, buying potential, or other relevant considerations.

- An area may be growing so quickly that your current distributor is simply no longer in a position to service the market adequately. In any event, the addition of new distributors in existing territories needs considerable thought and diplomacy. Be aware, however, your motive for maximizing territory coverage can prove counterproductive if it demoralizes your current distributors.

- Changes due to natural attrition, the death or retirement of principals, or the sale or collapse of a distributor are by far the most frequent reason for appointing new distributors.

Yet, more often than ever, erosion in your distributor mix comes about by inadequate distributor performance that leaves the manufacturer, or even both sides, dissatisfied. However, such a move can prove painful and disruptive and should be undertaken only in extreme cases. In some instances, you may try to rekindle an existing relationship, as long as there is a willingness to recognize the dynamic changes of the marketplace, and consequently the changes required in strategy.

Examining your distribution structure

Rarely should you have to revamp your entire distribution structure. In such a restructuring, you may add or eliminate an intermediary step in distributing your company's products, requiring the selection of new distributors.

If, on the other hand, you decide to make a change from direct to indirect distribution, you will have to build a national distributor network from scratch – a formidable challenge, requiring years of analysis, search, and organization.

Once you establish a need for new or additional distributor representation, your next task is to develop a list of candidates. You usually have a number of sources for this list, including your own field salesforce, your manager of distributor sales, trade associations, and present distributors and dealers.

The intelligent selection of distributive outlets for your firm requires more than the good judgment of a few key people. Since so much is at stake, the selection process should be directed by a set of carefully chosen guidelines consistently applied. These selection criteria have to be customized to suit the particular conditions and goals of your firm.

Table 10.2 highlights the selection criteria most often mentioned by some 200 leading manufacturers in a study on this subject. Look at how the numerous considerations are classified and summarized into a limited number of categories that can apply to any distributor selection task.

It is a monumental task to both formulate and apply a set of selection criteria suited to your particular circumstances. But it is well worth the effort, since it should lead to a satisfying, long-lasting relationship.

Selecting a distributor is by no means a one-way street. Rather, it is a matter of both sides choosing to work with each other. Thus, once you have made a selection, you have to persuade the prospect to join your team.

It may well be that your prospective distribution partner is scrutinizing your firm just as carefully. You should welcome that and be willing to supply information as freely as you expect to receive it. A well-analyzed commitment is bound to last longer than a hasty decision.

Criteria	Reasoning
Financial aspects	Only a distributor of solid financial strength and practices can assure you of adequate, continuous representation
Sales organization and performance	The sales strength and record of a prospect is essential to your potential relationship
Number of salespeople (in the field and on the inside)	The general rule: the more salespeople, the more sales and the more effective the market coverage
Sales and technical competence Sales performance	Salespeople with inadequate technical and sales skills are a liability A track record speaks for itself
Product lines carried Competitive products Compatible products Quality level Number of lines	Select your partners carefully Generally disdained, sometimes okay Tend to be beneficial The higher, the better Will your line get enough attention
Reputation	You are judged by the company you keep
Market coverage Geographic coverage Industry coverage Intensity of coverage	Exposure means sales Avoid overlap and conflicts Major user groups must be covered Infrequent calls mean lost business
Inventory and warehousing Kind and size of inventory Warehousing facilities	Ability to deliver is often crucial You want the right mix and a willingness to maintain adequate stock Storage and handling must be appropriate
Management Ability Continuity Attitudes	Proper leadership spells success You want competent leadership Succession should be assured Look for enthusiasm and aggressiveness

Table 10.2: Criteria for selecting distributors

Evaluating distributors

Once you have secured the services of a distributor candidate, you must then ensure that your association brings maximum benefit to both parties.

You need to perform periodic evaluations designed to keep you continually informed about the relative performance of your various distributors.

These evaluations may be in the nature of current operating appraisals or may take on the form of overall performance reviews. If they are simple and limited in scope, you could conduct them monthly. Thorough analyses, however, should be undertaken only at infrequent intervals: annually, biannually, or even triannually.

Use the following guidelines:

- If you engage in selective rather than exclusive distribution, the amount of evaluative input that you can readily obtain from your distributors is quite limited, forcing you to rely mostly on your own records, observations, and intelligence.

- If your product is a high-volume, low-cost item with little need for after-sale servicing, you can restrict yourself to a more limited evaluation than in the case of complex systems installations.

- If your team is composed of many hundreds of multi-line distributors, you will tend to take a closer look at a particular reseller only if its sales trends are way out of line. This procedure is called 'evaluation by exception'.

- If your firm employs only a moderate number of outlets, your analysis can be more thorough.

Whatever you conclude from your evaluation, it will rarely result in the termination of a particular distributor's services. Elimination is truly the last step, after all attempts to re-establish a satisfactory relationship have failed. The expense, time, and trouble involved in dropping a distributor and appointing an established outlet or even appointing an additional distributor are considerably less appealing alternatives.

The following case summarizes the new waves of distribution by illustrating how one company integrates distribution into a competitive strategy.

Owens & Minor

A distributor of hospital supplies, Owens & Minor, typifies the emerging role of the middleman in the distribution channel. Combining technology and customer service as the centrepieces of its strategy, O&M has taken control of its channel.

Such a role traditionally belonged to manufacturers and they reinforced that viewpoint with, 'We can price it lower because we've eliminated the middleman.'

This has changed. Increasing numbers of distributors in a variety of industries are responding to customers' calls for help, having been pounded by intense competition and high operating costs that have put them in a cash bind.

How are distributors shaping their strategies? Let's break down Owens & Minor's activities into four categories:

1. **Inventory**. Owens & Minor's employees take a daily inventory at their customer hospitals using hand-held electronic devices linked to the hospitals' computers.

    The computers then transmit orders directly to its regional distribution centres where daily deliveries are scheduled. In one hospital, where this managed inventory system was installed, inventory that included everything from catheters to rubbish bags, once valued at $306,000 was reduced to around $60,600. With cash-strapped hospitals seeking relief, the managed-inventory system satisfies the customer, strengthens the distributor-buyer relationship, and gives O&M's strategy a commanding edge.

2. **Management efficiency**. With inventory control and just-in-time delivery, hospitals benefit further by less paperwork, fewer employees, less stockroom maintenance, and reduced spoilage from such products as baby formula. One customer estimated it saved $9 million in three years using the system.

3. **Consultation**. Besides reducing inventories, O&M advises its customers on ways to reduce waste. In one instance, its personnel observed that a hospital was spending $736 on products for each open-heart operation, compared with $516 spent by other customers for the same procedure. Altering the contents of one sterilized package saved that hospital the difference.

4. **Growth**. With an efficient distribution system in place, O&M managers capitalize on their dominance by adding products to their line. This generates more profitable sales volume with only incremental costs, while satisfying customers with one-stop-shopping.

Action strategy

What can you learn from the Owens & Minor case, whether you are a distributor or manufacturer?

If you are a distributor:

Take control of the distribution channel by becoming more than just a conduit for supplying products from manufacturer to customer. Utilize technology to manage customers' inventories, improve delivery times, solve customers' problems related to waste, and reduce costs in order processing and shipping.

If you are a manufacturer:

Recognize that if you decide to bypass the middleman, you will have to deliver the above services. With distributors taking the initiative, it may be a prudent alternative to select a distributor and provide maximum support, even to the extent of supplying capital to purchase or update the distributor's technology. Such an alliance accepts the middlemen not as a weak link in a distribution chain, but as a powerful coupling to activate a marketing strategy.

Regardless of your position in the distribution chain, there are key functions you have to deal with in shaping a distribution strategy:

- **Information**: Collect, analyze, and disseminate market intelligence about potential and current customers, competitors, and other forces affecting the market.

- **Communication**: Combine various forms of communication including literature, videos, and workshops to attract and retain customers.

- **Negotiation**: Seek agreement on price, terms of delivery, and other value-added services as they relate to a preferred-customer status and long-term relationship.

- **Ordering**: Set-up procedures for the efficient electronic transmission of ordering information, e.g. using the Internet.

- **Financing**: Develop the means to fund a managed inventory system, similar to Owens & Minor.

- **Risk taking**: Assume the responsibility for risks associated with the expanded middleman activities.

- **Physical possession**: Develop the capability to store additional varieties of products for customers and manage increases in inventory turnover.

- **Payment**: Design an effective system for payment – including the selective financing of inventories for the buyer.

- **Title**: Develop a system to pinpoint the transfer of ownership from seller to buyer. In some situations, inventory is held at the buyer's location and title changes only when usage occurs.

With the backward and forward flow of activities throughout the supply chain, different participants in the channel assume distinct functions. Therefore, whether manufacturer or distributor, when forming a relationship clearly define the role of each channel member.

Best practices

Before converting your distribution strategies into action, remember that excessive distance and time between your product and its availability to customers adds a burden to an operation. Shorten the length of the distribution channel and reduce the communication time between the customer and the home office to assure profitable market conditions.

To identify strategies and initiate action:

1. List the distribution strategies that will represent the best opportunities.

2. Indicate what actions are to take place and which personnel would be assigned the tasks.

3. Obtain feedback and relate it to the objectives desired and the strategies selected.

4. List immediate plans and future courses of action.

11

How to think like a strategist

Chapter objectives

Leadership and implementing strategy

Relationship marketing

Align marketing strategy with your corporate culture

Benchmarking for success

Think like a strategist

Best practices

Chapter objectives

After reading this chapter you should be able to:

- Define the leadership role of the manager in implementing competitive marketing strategies.

- Determine how to use relationship marketing for optimum efficiency in a customer-driven marketplace.

- Align marketing strategy with your corporate culture.

- Install procedures to benchmark your marketing strategy and improve performance.

- Learn to think like a strategist.

The full impact of the Internet age has hit numerous managers who have been rudely jolted to learn that nurturing customer relationships, staying close to evolving technologies, developing strategic marketing plans, and devising bold competitive strategies that involve e-commerce are more than routine activities and academic truisms. They become organizational imperatives for survival.

Also, in a relatively short span of time, other managers have been hurled into a market scene where impetuous start-up companies have left the traditional market leaders in a cloud of dust.

Consequently, many of the awakened managers have learned the hard way to react with skill and competence to the sudden appearance of aggressive competitors from developing countries in Asia and Eastern Europe. They have also internalized the evolving applications of e-commerce and adapted to vast changes in communications technology.

Above all, within that maze of internal and external market conditions, managers are expanding their ability to perform as effective leaders. Meaning: They are honing skills to be able to react rapidly to industry changes, develop response strategies to counter sudden competitive actions – and lead others to willingly implement marketing strategies.

Leadership and implementing strategy

Your best strategy cannot produce good results if your short-term tactics – those actions that are in the minds and hands of your front-line personnel to implement – are flawed by negative mindsets and behaviour.

It is at this critical juncture that your confidence as a leader and manager must show through. Not just with animated and transparent confidence. Rather, with intimate, firm, conscious confidence, which can fire-up employees to act with sustained energy, and doesn't disappear at the moment of competitive tension.

It is not difficult to see that individuals move by emotion, strength, and courage in the face of pressure. However, if there is a lack of discipline; or if they are not suitably trained; or if solid support is withheld by the organization, your personnel will be overwhelmed by a competitor whose employees may be individually less brave, but as a unified group firmly organized, trained, and disciplined.

Organizational solidarity and confidence cannot be improvised. They are formed of mutual respect and acquaintanceship, which establishes pride and makes for unity. And from unity comes the feeling of energy. In turn, it gives to the human effort the courage and confidence of success. Thus, the cliché 'all for one and one for all' remains solidly valid.

Courage and unity, then, are the core ingredients that dominate the will over instinct, especially where the stakes get down to winning or losing. Therein lies the justification for forming strategy teams.

To function as a leader means influencing people by providing purpose, direction, and motivation, while improving the viability of the organization. Therefore, if you are responsible for supervising people and implementing marketing strategies that involve deploying resources, you are a leader.

Within that framework, you need to develop a personalized, yet flexible leadership style. Anything else will come across to your personnel as artificial and insincere. This is especially important if you expect them to support your overall marketing plan.

Also, if you rely on only one leadership style, you suffer the consequences of being rigid and will likely experience difficulty operating in situations where a single style simply doesn't work. That is, some projects are complex and require different management skills at each stage of development.

For instance, plans in the early stages of development, where creative insight and patient discussions among staff dominate, require a far different leadership style from that of pumping-up a salesforce when launching a new product.

Similarly, products at various stages of their life cycles – introduction, growth, maturity, decline, and phase-out – involve different leadership styles to correspond to the varying market and competitive conditions at each stage.

For those reasons, there is no single leadership style for all occasions. Therefore, shape a leadership style that fits your organization's overall climate. Be certain, however, that it conforms to the specific tasks you require to be performed.

Also be clear in your mind that your style measures up to the way personnel feel about the climate that exists in your organization. Meaning: Climate is composed of employees' common perceptions and attitudes and what they believe about the day-to-day functioning of the organization and their respective units.

Climate is also allied with corporate culture. Therefore, if you are to develop realistic strategies and implement them to a successful conclusion, it is in your best interest to define the environment in which you work. (See following discussion on aligning marketing strategy to corporate culture.)

Accordingly, answer the following questions to determine your organization's climate and your role in it. Although you may not be in a position to make changes, at least you can point to the negatives and positives that exist in the everyday workings of the organization and thereby personalize your own leadership style.

- Are priorities and goals clearly stated and do your personnel generally accept them?

- Is there a workable system of recognition, rewards, and reprimands? Does it work?

- Do you seek input from subordinates? And do you act on the feedback provided? In particular, do you keep your people informed?

- In the absence of instructions, do individuals reporting to you have authority to make decisions that are consistent with your objectives? Do they take the initiative and act in times of opportunity or emergency?

- Are there signs of high levels of stress and negative competition in the organization? What are the causes?

- Is your leadership style consistent with your company's
values? Is there a working climate of trust? Do other leaders
make good role models?

Overall, leadership means assessing a market and competitive situation, looking for opportunities, developing strategies and tactical
plans, and implementing them. It requires leadership in setting
performance standards, motivating personnel to discover for
themselves what happened, why something happened, and how to
sustain strengths and improve on weaknesses.

Qualities of successful leaders

Individuals enter an organization with a personal set of values, developed and nurtured from childhood through lifetime experiences.
In varying degrees, these values are expressed as loyalty, duty,
respect, and integrity.

However, they are empty qualities and may not fully surface if their
personal behaviours do not mesh with the organization's values,
customs, ethics, rules, and other patterns of behaviour. Where an
interconnect does take place, the leader, through words, deeds, and
everyday practices, communicates *purpose*, provides *direction*, instills
motivation, hones *skills*, and delivers *action*.

For example:

- *Purpose* gives people a reason to do things.

- *Direction* means prioritizing tasks, assigning responsibility
for completing them, and making sure personnel understand
the goals. The aim is also to deploy resources for the best
outcome.

- *Motivation* inspires personnel to act on their own initiative
when they see something that needs to be done – that is, within
the overall guidelines of business objectives.

- *Skills* relates to knowledge of people and how to work with
them, ability to understand and apply company policies and
guidelines to do the job, and technical competence to use the
required tools and techniques.

Relationship marketing

Central to the new-wave business practices is relationship marketing.

Relationship marketing is the practice of building long-term satisfying relations with key parties – customers, suppliers, distributors – in order to retain their long-term preference and business.

The intent is to deliver high quality, distinctive service, and competitive prices to customers. The pledge is to cut down on activity costs and time. Cisco Systems, cited in Chapter 1, is a prime example of a company that is a model for carrying out relationship marketing.

Relationships can run the gamut from an almost non-existent one of a salesperson simply selling a product, to that of a flourishing relationship where partnering means working consistently with a customer to discover ways to generate customer savings. Or it can mean helping the customer design a product for its customers. In some instances relationships can include placing an individual on the customer's premises to assist in a variety of tasks from inventory control to providing technical assistance.

Thus, the movement is to evolve from transaction marketing to relationship marketing. To implement the transition, your approach is to track customers and determine which ones are worthy of the full services of relationship marketing. Therefore:

- Identify the key customers warranting relationship marketing.

- Train the salesperson or other contact individual to deal with the customer.

- Require that a customer-relationship plan detail the objectives, actions, and required resources to implement the programme.

- Make the Internet and related technology an integral part of the marketing relationship plan.

In keeping with the aims of relationship marketing, there are distinct benefits for including the Internet. For instance, Office Depot reports the following tangible cost advantages and additional customer support for its office supply business:

- The Internet cuts in half the cost of processing an order. Typically, it costs about $2.40 to process a phone order, but over the Web that drops to less than $1.20.

- Office Depot has won new customers who are not close to its store and who now use the company's website to order goods.

- The company is able to hold on to its customers. Those that might depart to on-line competitors now stay with Office Depot.

- Business people can place orders from their desks and reduce phone calls to the purchasing department.

- Customers can get an up-to-the-minute review into Office Depot's extensive inventory, order what they want and state when they want delivery, thereby doing away with or reducing the amount of supplies they maintain on their own premises.

Align marketing strategy with your corporate culture

Aligning your business strategies with your corporate culture is precisely what will give your plan the singular quality of uniqueness. In practical day-to-day terms, synchronizing strategies with culture will directly impact the markets you focus on, the image you project in the marketplace, the products and services you deliver, and the competitors you are able to face up to successfully.

From a leadership and marketing strategy viewpoint: If you know how to identify the power of your corporate culture, you will get an unmistakable signal whether your strategies can work under adverse competitive conditions. It also provides useful insights about the success or failure of your entire marketing plan.

Consider these points at various levels within an organization:

- If you are a senior executive or business owner who consciously integrates your business strategy with the organization's culture, you are more likely to achieve your objectives.

- If you are a middle manager at the division, department, or product-line level who knows how to write a marketing plan that builds on the sub-culture of your business unit, you are more likely to win.

- If you do not internalize how the culture of the organization interweaves with today's hotly contested markets and do not know how to align your strategies accordingly, the results can prove fatal.

If you recognize that corporate culture envelop your entire organization, such as: the calibre of leadership, the vision that drives the business plan, the boldness or timidity of strategies, the commitment to customers' needs and problems, and the care and treatment of employees, then you are more likely to succeed.

Characteristics of high-performing business cultures

Corporate culture, then, is the DNA that is implanted in your strategies. It permeates day-to-day organizational life. It functions as the critical lifeline to your organization's future. It delineates, and delimits, the types and range of strategies you can realistically undertake, and provides some measure of assurance that you will realize your objectives.

Corporate culture spans the extreme boundaries of growth or retreat, viability or stagnation, or in its extreme, survival or bankruptcy. To grasp the underlying nature of your organization's culture and to internalize what makes your organization tick is to foretell whether your plans have a reasonable chance of succeeding.

General Electric Co. CEO Jeffrey Immelt indicated his concerns when he declared, "I'm intense about our competition. But I'm more concerned about our culture and our people." He further defined his fears: first, that GE would become boring; second, that his top people might act out of fear. Meaning: Some executives would shy away from taking the essential risks to propel the company forward.

Accordingly, if you take the time to sort through the core values, deep-seated beliefs, and historical traditions that shape your organization's culture, you can control how successful you will be in running your operation. Such awareness is one of the primary steps when formulating a business strategy. Doing so also strengthens your ability to engage the minds and hearts of the personnel who must take responsibility for its implementation. As a tangible outcome of that effort, you will be able to develop more exacting marketing strategies and tactics that can win in hotly contested markets.

Corporate culture consists of the deep-rooted traditions, values, beliefs, and history that power the organization and drive individuals' actions. It is dynamic. It is never static. It forms the backbone of your business strategy.

Accordingly, there is no generically good culture as there is no one-size-fits-all marketing strategy. However, there are six universal attributes that sustain a competitively healthy corporate culture, whereby individuals:

1. Respond rapidly to changing market conditions.

2. Exploit fresh opportunities with a bold and unified approach.

3. Strengthen customer relationships as an ongoing corporate imperative.

4. Create innovative products and services based on a blend of creativity and technology.

5. Adhere to the rules of competitive strategy.

6. React to their leadership with high morale and by nurturing their personal and professional growth.

In contrast, a staid and uninspiring corporate culture closes its eyes to global competition, vacillates over the competitive impact of new technologies, focuses only on building market share in existing markets rather than pushing the boundaries of new markets, and is generally passive to changing buying trends.

Additional negative signs include a conscious disregard for making its corporate culture compatible with a constantly changing marketplace. Result: The organization loses its edge, complacency spreads, customer focus declines, and originality dries up.

Therefore, a positive, supportive corporate culture drives ambitious business decisions, generates customer loyalty, and ignites employee involvement. You can count on the following five underlying elements to sustain a supportive corporate culture: *Fairness, openness, independence, resilience, and entrepreneurship.*

These elements, then, become the winning performance combination for a forward-looking corporate culture and the platform for winning leadership. Further, for you to operate successfully in a constructive corporate culture means tuning-in to your firm's basic beliefs, moral codes, traditions, and standards. This approach will work for you as long as the underpinnings of your organization's or business unit's culture harmonize with the current competitive environment and your firm's aspirations.

Therefore, aligning your marketing strategies with your corporate culture is precisely what will give your plan the singular quality of uniqueness. In practical day-to-day terms, synchronizing strategies with culture will directly impact the markets you focus on, the image you project in the marketplace, the products and services you deliver, and the competitors you are able to face up to successfully.

From a leadership and managerial viewpoint: If you know how to identify the power of your corporate culture, you will get an unmistakable signal whether your strategies can work under adverse competitive conditions. It also provides useful insights about the success or failure of your entire business plan.

The following guidelines will permit you to compare the key characteristics of successful corporate cultures with your own.

Beliefs and values:

- Total commitment to customer satisfaction.
- Openness to new ideas.
- Tolerance for diversity.
- Respect for individuals' achievements.
- Ethical conduct.
- Personal fulfillment.

Employee treatment and expectations:

- Fairness with discipline.
- Independence with an entrepreneurial outlook.
- Resilience with personal growth.
- Continuous learning.
- Employee motivation.
- High morale and pride in the organization.

Organizational structure:

- Use of cross-functional teams to cultivate originality and innovation.
- Rapid internal communications through a flat organization.
- Speed of decision-making.
- Mutually supportive internal relationships.
- Increased authority and responsibility at the field sales level.

Leadership and implementing strategy:

- Skill in implementing marketing strategies and tactics.
- Maximum use of competitive intelligence.
- Alignment of culture with strategy.
- Sensitivity to market changes.
- Focus on customer retention.
- Emphasis on leadership competence.

Vision and managerial competence:

- Expertise in strategic marketing planning.

- Vision to locate new and evolving market opportunities.

- Ability to nurture the health and vibrancy of the organization or your business unit.

- Aptitude to conceptualize and communicate a market-driven direction.

- Facility to convert vision to action.

- Sensitivity and diplomacy to develop and maintain cooperative external relationships.

In sum, the overall culture of an organization, or its individual business units and product lines, incarnates the core beliefs and values that drive business decisions, generate customer loyalty, and ignite employee involvement.

Benchmarking for success

Underlying this and previous chapters are the vital inputs of market research and competitor intelligence into the development of your marketing strategies. However, to test the validity of your strategy in the competitive arena, there is still one more procedure needed to assure your success: Establishing a process for continuous tracking by benchmarking.

Still fairly new to many organizations, benchmarking consists of systematic and continuous assessments that compare and measure a firm's business processes against those of business leaders anywhere in the world.

One key outcome of benchmarking is information that would permit you to re-examine your operations, re-assess traditional methods, and learn how and why some companies perform with greater success than others inside and outside their industries. Such information helps initiate actions to improve performance in areas critical to success.

Conducting a competitive benchmarking study provides the following benefits:

- Improves your understanding of customers' needs and sensitizes you to the underlying dynamics operating within your industry.

- Helps you document which organizations can perform similar processes at a higher performance level than your own.

- Creates a sense of urgency for you to develop long-term improvement and performance objectives.

- Encourages a spirit of competitiveness as managers recognize that performance levels among best-in-class organizations may exceed their own perceptions of exceptional performance.

- Motivates individuals to strive to new heights of innovative thinking and achievement.

Xerox Corporation is an outstanding example of successful benchmarking. Hit hard during the early 1980s by intense Japanese competitors, it made a successful turnaround and regained substantial market share. Many factors contributed to the about-face. Among them was a process of using twelve success factors for conducting a competitive benchmarking study. Table 11.1 outlines these factors, which are broad enough to apply to most organizations.

Planning	Analysis	Implementation
1. Identify benchmark outputs	4. Determine current competitive 'gap'	7. Establish functional goals
2. Identify best competitor	5. Project future performance levels	8. Implement specific actions
3. Determine data collection method	6. Develop functional action plans	9. Monitor results and report progress
		10. Recalibrate benchmarks
		11. Obtain leadership position
		12. Integrate processes fully in business practice

Table 11.1: Competitive benchmarking actions

Benchmarking is not a stand-alone activity. Particularly in the Internet age, it is firmly linked to the hallmarks of solid management practices, with emphasis on quality of output and primary attention to the customer.

In turn, this linkage translates into three pragmatic guidelines essential in any competitive encounter:

- Develop quality beyond that of competitors.

- Harness technology before competitors.

- Keep costs below those of competitors.

Benchmarking seeks to transform those guidelines into a set of procedures leading to customer satisfaction. In turn, they serve as the strategies to capture and maintain market share.

How do you get started? Implementing benchmarking requires three basic ingredients:

1. A supportive management group.

2. Access to prospective benchmarking partners who have previously addressed a competitive problem you are facing.

3. A benchmarking team with the ability to use reliable research practices to investigate the root cause of your problem.

Keep in mind, however, the benchmarking process is more than just conducting a competitive analysis – a practice that has been emphasized throughout this book. Rather, benchmarking aims to assist an organization – such as yours – in developing superior marketing strategies and improving overall performance. (If benchmarking is already underway in your group, the next step is to further refine measurements that result in a deeper understanding of competitors' cultures, attitudes, and business practices.)

Think like a strategist

Managing marketing strategies in the Internet age with its dazzling technology and rapid communications has become the centrepiece of management practice. Yet, the assorted activities associated with implementing strategies invariably lean heavily on fundamental marketing concepts, techniques, and practices that have evolved during the last half of the 20th century. For instance, developing a market-driven, customer-orientation and getting closer to the customer are time-honoured concepts of modern marketing, but only now can they be fully implemented with the use of Internet technology.

What follows, then, are guidelines for honing your skills to think like a strategist. Initially, your task is to establish a set of core values, concepts, and a framework that can guide you in operating your business in the 21st century. Use the following criteria for constructing the underpinnings of your strategies and for developing a pattern of thinking:

- **Leadership**: Observe how you and your organization's executives address core values and performance expectations, and how you focus on and create value for customers. Look at how you and other managers set directions and seek future opportunities for your organization. As important (and strongly emphasized in this book), consider the level of leadership displayed in developing innovative strategies that would improve your company's competitive performance.

- **Strategic marketing planning**: Examine your organization's strategy development process, including how your organization develops a strategic direction, objectives, strategies, and a business portfolio. (Review Chapter 5, How to manage your strategic marketing plan.)

  The plan is a vital document. In addition to competitive strategies, the output should also highlight where you would develop or improve various capabilities, such as a swift response to customer requests, market intelligence, customer relationships, rapid product innovation, technology management, and information management.

- **Customer and market focus**: Look at how your organization determines customer and market requirements, expectations, and preferences. Look, too, at how your organization builds relationships with customers and determines their level of satisfaction. Also, observe how you decide on target customers, customer groups, and/or market segments.

  This focus translates to the attention you give to product features that bear upon customer preference and re-purchase loyalty. Also, features might include price, value, delivery, customer or technical support, sales relationships, and any innovations that would differentiate your products and services from competing offerings.

- **Customer satisfaction and relationships**: Determine how your organization harnesses customer relationships, not only to retain current business but to develop new market and product opportunities. Here, look at such areas as key customer contact requirements, how you ensure that complaints are resolved effectively and promptly, and how you build high levels of satisfaction with your customers for repeat business and/or positive referrals.

- **Information and analysis**: Review the systems you use to analyze your organization's performance data and information – as well as intelligence about your customers and competitors. Then use the data to establish signposts that will alert you to dangers as well as opportunities.

- **Human resource focus**: Look at how your organization encourages your employees to develop and utilize their full potential. The central idea here is that your strategy fundamentally boils down to the mind of one manager pitted against the mind of a competing manager. Consequently, you want your team composed of individuals who are motivated to design and execute strategies using well-developed skills. The goal is for each individual to think and act like a strategist – and benchmark these strategies to high-level performance.

- **Process management**: Review the key aspects of your organization's process management, involving all work units. This survey should cover customer-focused design, product and service delivery, and technical support.

- **Business results**: Examine your overall organization's performance in key business areas: customer satisfaction, product and service performance, financial and marketplace performance, human resource results, supplier and partner networking results, and operational performance. These same areas should also be examined for performance levels relative to competitors.

Best practices

The following list summarizes the best of the key concepts and techniques to help you think like a strategist:

1. First and foremost, focus on your customer. Build your organization on change, not stability. Organize around networks connecting customers, suppliers, business partners, and employees. Develop a corporate culture that leads to healthy relationships, not only with customers and suppliers, but also with an attitude about employees as intellectual assets.

   Keep in mind the definition of marketing used in this book:

   Marketing is a total system of interacting business activities designed to plan, price, promote, and distribute want-satisfying

249

products or services to organizational and household users in a competitive environment at a profit.

2. Recognize that the Internet should now become an integral part of your marketing strategy. Its advantages of fewer capital assets, a direct-to-customer connection, and freedom from the formal management structure offer a new level of speed and operational efficiency.

3. Utilize strategy teams made up of various functional managers. The team is not a temporary ad hoc committee but a permanent part of the organizational framework and applicable to all sizes and levels of organizations.

4. A core concept of strategy is that no manager is justified in launching a sales and marketing campaign against a competitor that is entrenched in an actively defended market-leader position. Consequently, if there is little or no differentiation in such areas as product, promotion, pricing, or distribution (the marketing mix), there is minimal chance of success. Further, an effective strategy is to concentrate in those market segments that are emerging, neglected, or poorly served by competitors.

   The underlying intent here is to internalize strategy's ultimate purpose: *the reduction of resistance*. Do so by implementing the five principles of strategy – speed, indirect approach, concentration, alternative objectives, and unbalancing the competition.

5. Competitive analysis is the central activity for understanding your market, assessing competitors' intentions and strategies, launching into new markets, and determining how customers respond to your offerings versus those of your competitors. More precisely, there is no practical approach to designing a winning strategy without the input of reliable and documented competitive intelligence.

   The World Wide Web is now the trigger for the explosive level of activity to acquire huge quantities of finite information, not only about group behaviour but also of individuals. Keep in mind, however, that market intelligence systems are not used with the intention of replacing people. Their central purpose is to improve decision-making.

6. Planning remains the indispensable duty and responsibility of managers at all levels of authority. Reason: firms with written plans grow faster, achieve a higher proportion of revenues from new products and services, and enable chief executives to manage more critical business functions than those firms whose plans are unwritten. Thus, strategic marketing planning sets in motion actions that can impact the long-term prosperity of your organization.

7. Segmenting the market helps you identify and satisfy the specific needs of targeted groups, which results in strengthening your market position. You can identify market segments by dividing a market into groups of customers with common characteristics. Segmentation also allows you to concentrate your strength against the weaknesses of your competitors, at which point you can improve your competitive ranking.

8. Use the product life cycle to provide a reliable perspective for observing a 'living' product moving through dynamic stages. The classic product life cycle pattern conforms reasonably well to reality and remains a pragmatic and useful tool to monitor your product's sales life.

   Different conditions characterize the stages of the product life cycle, and are influenced by outside economic, social, and environmental forces, as well as by inside policies, priorities, and available resources. Using the marketing mix as your format, your job is to develop strategies that extend the sales life of products.

9. New products and services are the heart of any business that seeks to sustain growth and competitive advantage. Since a new product is considered new when it is *perceived* as new by the prospective buyer, you can tap five categories of new products: modification, line extension, diversification, remerchandizing, and market extension.

10. Effective use of promotion can force competitors to react to *your* moves on your terms. For instance, the timing of your promotion can weaken competitors by making them use additional resources after they have completed a major sales promotion effort. To initiate action: list the advertising, sales promotion, and Internet objectives that represent the best opportunities and integrate them into your marketing mix.

11. The ultimate success of your marketing depends on moving your product to its intended market. Accordingly, you should

take considerable care in selecting distribution strategies and consider the far-reaching impact of the complete supply chain.

Before converting your distribution strategies into action, remember that excessive distance and time between your product and its availability to customers, adds a burden to an operation. Therefore, shorten the length of the distribution channel and reduce communication time between the customer and the home office to assure profitable market conditions.

Putting these practices into action will lessen the risk of failure and will go a long way to assure your success in this remarkable era of the Internet age. Good luck!

Other titles from Thorogood

GURUS ON MARKETING

Sultan Kermally

Paperback £14.99
ISBN: 978-185418243-2
Ringbound £24.99
ISBN: 978-185418238-8

A one-stop guide to the world's most influential writers on marketing, their key concepts, theories and frameworks. Includes Drucker, Levitt on 'marketing myopia', Kotler on marketing management, Porter on competitive strategy, Day, Nagle, Ansoff, Seth and Peters.

THE PR PRACTITIONER'S DESKTOP GUIDE

Caroline Black

Paperback £16.99
ISBN: 978-185418260-9
Ringbound £55.00
ISBN: 978-185418265-4

A practical source of reference on every aspect of the business written by a successful PR professional, clearly laid out and packed with valuable checklists, tips and techniques, warning signs and helpful summaries.

WIN NEW BUSINESS – THE DESKTOP GUIDE

Susan Croft

Paperback £16.99
ISBN: 978-185418290-6
Ringbound £55.00
ISBN: 978-185418295-1

A comprehensive guide to the techniques of developing new business, by a professional with extensive experience of both Europe and the USA.

"This book has an excellent and logical structure with a clear and cogent writing style. It is a thorough primer for people in sales and business development and I commend it as such."

JOHN DALTON, DIRECTOR, LONDON SCHOOL
OF PUBLIC RELATIONS

"This comprehensive and practical guide is packed with invaluable information and advice that will benefit you both professionally and personally. Hats off to Susan Croft for a well written and very interesting book! This should be on every business owner's bookshelf!"

PATRICIA NAMEISHI, CEO, MARKETING CONCEPTS ASIA

THE MANAGER'S GUIDE TO COMPETITIVE MARKETING STRATEGIES

Norton Paley

Paperback £16.99
ISBN: 978-185418365-1
Hardback £29.99
ISBN: 978-185418370-5

The third edition of this best-selling book includes new sections on corporate culture, business intelligence, CRM and leadership, as well as many brand new case studies reflecting current issues including: assessing corporate culture and turning it into competitive advantage, manoeuvring around competitors when trapped in a weak position, energising a product line and reviving a business after a period of no-growth.

MARKETING YOUR SERVICE BUSINESS

Ian Ruskin-Brown

Paperback £15.99
ISBN: 978-185418316-3
Hardback £24.99
ISBN: 978-185418311-8

"An enlightening and rewarding read... All the nuances of segmentation, positioning, pricing, promotion, service delivery and gaining customer feedback in a services context are explored, and Ruskin-Brown even adds a couple of new elements to the mix – time and resources... The book is aimed squarely at the practitioner and is full of useful case studies... those looking for expert advice on marketing their service business or using services to gain a competitive advantage need look no further than this accessible and useful guide."

THE MARKETER

"Those looking for expert advice on marketing their service business or using services to gain a competitive advantage, need look no further than this accessible and useful guide."

EXPAND YOUR SERVICE

MASTERING MARKETING

Ian Ruskin-Brown

Paperback, 2nd edition £15.99
ISBN: 978-185418323-1
Hardback £22.00
ISBN: 978-185418118-3

The ideal book for anyone seeking an introduction to marketing that is both comprehensive and accessible: all the key concepts, skills and techniques backed up by a wealth of examples and real life case studies which make the concepts instantly meaningful.

OUT OF THE BOX MARKETING

David Abingdon

Paperback £9.99
ISBN: 978-185418312-5

This treasure trove of a book is crammed full of time-tested strategies and techniques to help you to get more customers, get more out of your customers and to keep them coming back for more.

"David Abingdon is certainly an 'out of the box' marketing phenomenon! In the almost ten years I have known him he has built three multi-million pound sterling organisations from scratch, using the methodologies and precepts in this new book. His writings are simple and straight forward, yet extremely powerful."

DAN PENA, BUSINESS MENTOR & CHAIRMAN,
THE GUTHRIE GROUP

"You'd better read this book before your competitors do!"

PETER SUN, M.D., AUSTRALIA'S MARKETEER &
BETTER BUSINESS INSTITUTE

SUCCESSFUL SELLING SOLUTIONS

Julian Clay

Paperback £14.99
ISBN: 978-185418242-5
Hardback £22.99
ISBN: 978-185418298-2

This book goes beyond mere sales techniques: using self-assessment models, it shows you how to monitor your progress in an actual sales project against where you need to be and includes templates, tables and exercises.

Thorogood also has an extensive range of reports and special briefings which are written specifically for professionals wanting expert information.

For a full listing of all Thorogood publications, or to order any title, please call Thorogood Customer Services on 020 7749 4748 or fax on 020 7729 6110. Alternatively view our website at www.thorogoodpublishing.co.uk.